LOCKED DOWN, COOKIN'

CALVIN BROWN

Freebird Publishers

www.FreebirdPublishers.com

Freebird Publishers

221 Pearl St., Ste. 541 North Dighton, MA 02764
Info@FreebirdPublishers.com
www.FreebirdPublishers.com

All Freebird Publishers titles, imprints, and distributed lines are available at special quantity discounts for bulk purchases for sales promotions, premiums, fundraising, educational, or institutional use.

ISBN: 978-1-952159-06-0

Printed in the United States of America

This book was inspired by my three beautiful daughters, my granddaughter, grandson, family, and friends – including so many that are doing and have done time – and all those who enjoy eating great-tasting food.

The dedication goes to the three women whose instruction constitutes my certification in cooking: My grandmothers, Mrs. Magnolia Rouse and Mrs. Cornelius "Pig" Brown, and my mother, Mrs. Leola Rouse Dalton (LeLo).

Contents

Introduction

The recipes in this book come from my culinary knowledge and creativity; they are my own original recipes, and they have been a blessing to me in making people happy through my cooking. Each has been prepared repeatedly until perfected. Measurements are not a big thing in these recipes, and that's what makes them so quick and easy.

The ingredients you'll find here come from the prison canteen lists and from meal trays served to prisoners. These low-budget foods are available on most prison canteens/commissaries /stores. You may need to substitute some ingredients if they are not available to you. Other ingredients may come from your own institution's dining hall or kitchen.

Know that you have to use what ingredients are available to you; just try to keep them similar to what you find in the recipes. If you are using this book in the free world, please refer to the canteen list in the back of the book for brand names and amounts.

You have to be creative when cooking. I took my own canteen list and said to myself, "Creativity, be free!" Then I used my culinary touch and taste buds to produce meals "The Big Cal Way."

In cooking, you must have a great deal of patience, as well as a gentle touch. One motto I have always employed while living in my own kitchen is: "Add less, to add more."

Those who know me have heard my four most famous words: "I don't reveal magic!" I can't say that any longer, because my magic is here in this book – these recipes truly are magical. Please, enjoy!

Calvin Brown

Rules and Instructions

The most important thing in cooking is cleanliness. Clean everything before each stage of the meal; it is the number one rule.

Instructions for popcorn bag frying:

You will find reference to "popcorn bag frying" in these pages. When you do, here is what's needed: 1 empty popcorn bag and a microwave.

(You can fry rice, Ramen, mac and cheese, potatoes with skins on, pork skins, garlic bread, and more. Anything that you want to become crispy or golden brown, you can make happen with popcorn bag frying.)

Step one: Shake out the bag, making sure there is no popcorn remaining.

Step two: Place your food item[s] into the bag and shake to mix.

Step three: Place the bag flat, laying it down on the side that the microwave hot plate is on (it's a gray square on the front of the bag).

Step four: On your first cooking, let it fry for two minutes with the bag closed. After that, pull the bag out of the microwave and shake well.

Step five: Now fry it for one minute at a time. After every minute, remove and shake. As you are shaking the contents, you will see them turning in color, browning more each time you heat the bag. Repeat this until you are content with the golden brownness of your food.

Step six: You can also add butter and seasoning to your fry bag and follow steps one through five.

Calvin Brown

PIZZA

EASY-PEEZZ POCKETS

Ingredients:

1 – pack of flour tortilla (6 pack)

1 – meat item: sausage, chicken, pepperoni, etc.

1 – cheese bar or squeeze cheese

pizza sauce or ketchup with seasoning

jalapeños

The Whip-Game:

Dice the meat, add jalapeños, and place in a bowl with enough pizza sauce to cover both. Cook for approximately 2 minutes. Warm up your tortillas, then place diced cheese or squeeze cheese on them and add two or three spoons of the meat and sauce mixture. Fold all four sides of the tortilla in, tucking them tightly. Wrap them in plastic or paper and warm to serving temperature. Now, enjoy these easy-peezz pockets.

SELF-MADE. HANDMADE PIZZA

Ingredients:

1 – 6-pack of tortillas

1 – bottle of pizza sauce

1 – one cheese bar and squeeze cheese

1 – pack of pepperoni

1 – summer sausage (pork, beef, or chicken)

The Whip-Game:

Lightly poke your tortillas with a fork, then spread butter or water on the surface of each. Heat in a microwave on paper until crispy on both sides. (Do these 30 seconds at a time, flipping until golden brown.) Next, spread pizza sauce on each tortilla "to your liking." Then place your meat and cheese in the order you like. Reheat for 20 to 50 seconds. You can stack these and have yourself a deep-dish handmade crispy pizza, the Big Cal way. Enjoy.

MONTANA'S SWEET AND SPICY PIZZA ROLLS

Ingredients:

1 – 6-pack of tortillas

1 – bag of rice

1 – pack of pepperoni

1 – cheese bar (hot)

1 – hot-and-spicy seasoning pack from Ramen

3 – tablespoons of sugar

2 – sweeteners

1 – tablespoon each of onion and garlic powder

1/2 a bottle of pizza sauce

Just under a quarter cup of pizza sauce and chopped jalapeños

(Makes 6 rolls)

The Whip-Game:

Place rice in a bowl and add enough hot water to cover the rice. Set the rice aside. Mix your sugar, hot-and-spicy seasoning pack, and tablespoons of onion and garlic powder together, and then stir them into the rice. Cut your cheese bar into slices. In a separate bowl, mix your chopped jalapeños and pizza sauce. Warm up your tortillas and place enough rice in the center of each to create a small bed. Next, place 2 or 3 spoons of pizza sauce and jalapeños on the beds of rice, and then add 4 to 6 slices of cheese, followed by 6 to 8 pepperoni slices. Fold in the sides, and then fold your tortilla halfway up, leaving yourself room to roll up these bad boys. Sit back and let your taste buds be rolled away. Enjoy.

MEXICAN STYLE STACKED HANDMADE PIZZA

Ingredients:

1 – 6-pack of tortillas

1 – cheese bar, shredded

1 – bag of refried beans and rice

1 – pack of pepperoni

1 – sausage log

1/2 – cup of chopped jalapeños

1/2 – cup of squeeze cheese

The Whip-Game:

Cut up your sausage log and cook for 1 minute and 30 seconds. Place your refried beans in a bowl, adding just enough water to cover. Lightly poke the tortillas with a fork and spread with butter or water. Heat in a microwave on paper until crispy on both sides. (Heat for 30 seconds at a time, flipping each time until golden brown.) Next, place your squeeze cheese on each tortilla, followed by applying some of your beans and rice. Top with more cheese, pepperonis, and sausages. The last thing to add will be your chopped jalapeños and the rest of your cheese. Stack them and enjoy.

PEANUT BUTTER AND JELLY BREAKFAST PIZZA

Ingredients:

1 – 6-pack of tortillas

6 – tablespoons of peanut butter

1/2 – bottle of jelly, any flavor

Things that can be added: crushed peanuts, crushed cookies, raisins, or hot chocolate

The Whip-Game:

Lightly poke your tortillas with a fork, and then rub some water on them. Heat your tortillas in the microwave on paper until crispy on both sides. (Do this in 30-second intervals, flipping each time until tortillas are golden brown.) Next, place a tablespoon of peanut butter on each tortilla, and then apply your jelly. Any other toppings you like can be added now. Reheat for 20 to 50 seconds. You can stack these and have yourself a deep-dish breakfast pizza, the Big Cal way. Enjoy.

CHICKEN

BAKED MACARONI AND CHEESE WITH CHICKEN AND SAUSAGE

Ingredients:

1 – box or pack of mac and cheese

1 – cheese bar and squeeze cheese

1 – chicken pouch

1 – sausage

1 – pack of slightly seasoned and browned snack crackers or breadcrumbs (brown in the microwave)

The Whip-Game:

Place mac and cheese into 6 cups of boiling water with 1 teaspoon of salt (optional). Boil for 7 to 10 minutes until macaroni is tender. Add in the cheese that comes in the box. Add in your chicken and uncooked sausage, with just enough squeeze cheese and the seasoning of your choice. Jalapeños are also good in this dish. After you've added these ingredients and cooked for three minutes, let them cool down for one minute. Next, take your cheese bar, cut it into nice squares, and mix it into the mac and cheese. Level out the food, and then place the rest of your cheese bar on top, adding your seasoned crackers or breadcrumbs. Cook for three more minutes. This meal will serve up to two people. Enjoy.

MACKEREL FLATS OR CHICKEN ROUNDS

Ingredients:

2 – bags of your favorite chips (optional)

1 or 2 pouches of mackerel or chicken

1 or 2 sleeves of crackers

7 to 10 butter pats

The Whip-Game:

With one pouch of fish or chicken, use one sleeve of crackers (the type of crackers is your choice), with two pouches, use two sleeves. Crush the crackers and mix in six tablespoons of butter. (As an option, you can also crush and add your favorite chips, but add another butter packet. You can also add jalapeños if you like.) Once everything is in a bowl, add water until it is wet enough to form a flat or round shape. Mix everything together well, then make your flats to the size and thickness of your liking. After that, you can use a popcorn, rice, or chip bag to cook them on. Cook on both sides for 50 seconds or until done to your liking. These flats will hit the spot: Bullseye. Enjoy.

CHEESE ENCHILADAS

Ingredients:

1 – 6-pack of tortillas

1 – tuna (adding an additional chicken pouch is optional)

1 – bag of rice

1 – bag of refried beans and rice

1 – cheese bar

1 – bottle of salsa

half a bottle of squeeze cheese

chopped jalapeños and onion

garlic powder

The Whip-Game:

*This recipe can be made with or without the tuna and chicken; however, if you do use tuna and chicken, read the last part of this recipe first.

Cut up your cheese bar into thin slices, cutting as many as you can. Chop up a quarter cup of jalapeños. Place your rice in a bowl with 1/2 of your chopped jalapeños and one tablespoon each of onion and garlic powder. Add just enough water to cover the rice. Put your beans and rice in another bowl, adding just enough water to cover them, and then stir. Add just enough of your salsa to keep the beans and rice loose. Add to your half-bottle of squeeze cheese a little water to loosen it to the point you can pour it on your enchiladas, but not runny. Stir your rice into your instant beans and rice. You may need to add some warm water to loosen it if it has thickened. Warm up the tortillas, placing 6 slices of cheese down in the center, side by side. Then add your rice, followed by your bean and rice mixture. Place 6 more slices of cheese on top of your filling. Do these one at a time, wrapping each and placing as many in a bowl as will fit comfortably under the lid. Place them with the open side facing up and pour on the rest of your salsa, followed by your squeeze cheese and the rest of your jalapeños.

*If using tuna and chicken, mix them together – they come pre-cooked, so additional cooking is not necessary. Add some of this mixture inside your enchiladas and place the rest on top, right before pouring on your squeeze cheese. Heat up for 2 minutes, with the lid on your bowl, and 1 minute with the lid off. Enjoy such goodness …

Calvin Brown

BBQ CHICKEN TURNOVERS WITH GARLIC BUTTER

Ingredients:

1 – 6-pack of tortillas

1 – chicken pouch

2 – Ramen soups, chicken flavor

10 – butter pats

15 – tablespoons of BBQ sauce

garlic powder and some chopped-up jalapeños. You will also need a piece of plastic or big chip bag.

The Whip-Game:

First, take 8 of your butter pats and mix them slowly and gently into some garlic powder, not causing the butter to melt, and then place them to the side. Next, crush both Ramen soups (as an option, you can fry them) and place them in a bowl, adding 1 chicken seasoning pack and 2 pats of butter. Cover with just enough hot water to cook until they become gummy in texture. To your chicken, add in the other chicken seasoning pack and chopped jalapeños, along with the BBQ sauce. Cook for 2 minutes. Warm your tortillas. Then dampen the entire tortilla with water. Split your chip bag down one side and lay out flat (or spread some plastic out) in order to place your tortillas on it. On each tortilla, add down one side some of your garlic butter, followed by some of your gummy chicken flavored Ramen, and then spreading on your BBQ chicken. Fold over your tortilla, pinching the edges (you may need to wet your fingers). Cook these on your bowl lid or microwave-safe plastic for 1 minute, on both sides, until they become firm. You can top it with your favorite cheese or sauce. Six of these will turn up your stomach's smile. Always enjoy.

16

CHICKEN AND CHEESE CHILI FLAVORED QUESADILLAS

Ingredients:

1 – 6-pack of tortillas

2 – chicken pouch

2 – cheese bars

1 – chili seasoning pack

1 – tablespoon of garlic powder

The Whip-Game:

Shred your cheese bars. Place your chicken in a bowl and then add your chili seasoning pack and 1 tablespoon of garlic powder. Mix until it forms a paste. Line each tortilla with the chicken and cheese mixture and then fold over. Microwave for 1 minute and 30 seconds. Enjoy these quick and good quesadillas.

CHICKEN AND CHEESE POCKETS

Ingredients:

1 – 6-pack of tortillas

2 – chicken pouches

1 – cheese bar or squeeze cheese

1/2 – cup of sliced jalapeños

The Whip-Game:

Place chicken in a bowl with sliced jalapeños. Cook for approximately 1 minute and 30 seconds. Warm the tortillas and top with cut cheese or squeeze cheese and two or three spoons of chicken and jalapeño mixture. Fold all four sides inward, tucking them tightly. You can wrap them in plastic or paper, which will help heat them evenly. Warm and enjoy these scrumptious chicken and cheese pockets.

CHICKEN AND RICE PIE

Ingredients:

1 – 1/2 sleeves of saltines

1 – tortilla

2 – bags of rice

2 – chicken pouches

1 – cheese bar

3 – tablespoons of onion powder

1 – tablespoons of garlic powder

8 – butter pats

1 – quarter cup of Slam Sweet and Hot Asian hot sauce (or 2 hot and spicy seasoning packs)

The Whip-Game:

Pie crust: Crush your saltine crackers into a fine powder and place them into a big bag. Add in 6 butters, 1 tablespoon of garlic powder, and 1 tablespoon of onion powder. Slowly knead warm water into the mix until you achieve a firm paste. Once you are able to form a ball with your paste, your crust dough is done. Close the bag tightly.

Chicken prep: Place your chicken, 1 tablespoon of onion powder, your Asian hot sauce, and 1 butter pat in a bowl, and mix well. In another bowl, place your rice, your last tablespoon of onion powder, and 1 butter pat to the side.

Press your paste into your bowl, coming up the sides to form the crust. Microwave for 2 minutes. In your crust layer, in your rice, then cheese slices, and then chicken. Cover with your tortilla and top with some Asian hot sauce. Microwave pie for 2-3 minutes. Cut in slices or just plain dig in! Enjoy.

TAMALES

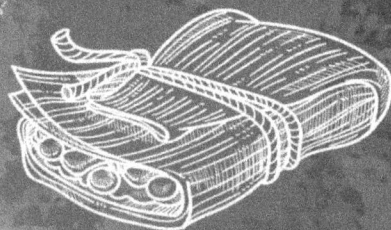

EASY CHEESE TAMALE BOWL

Ingredients:

3 – bags of Cheetos

1 – sausage

1 – chicken pouch

1 – cheese bar

1 – chili pouch

7 – butter pats

1 – bag of rice

onion and garlic powder

The Whip-Game:

In a bowl, mix your rice with one spoon each of your onion and garlic powder and 3 butter pats, and then add enough water to cover. Cut up your sausage on top of your rice. Add some chopped jalapeños. Cook for 1 minute, 30 seconds, and then add your chili pouch with just enough water to loosen. Cut up your cheese bar into nice-sized slices. Add onion and garlic powder to your chicken and mix well, but do not cook. Crush your Cheetos into a fine powder. Pour all 3 bags of crushed Cheetos into a bowl with 4 pats of butter and slowly add water while mixing, until it forms a paste. In another bowl, take your paste and make a layer. You should be able to make 3 layers out of your paste mixture. To your first layer of paste, add a layer of your rice. Next, lay down some of your cheese slices, then a layer of your chicken, then pour on a layer of chili, and finally a layer of sausage and jalapeños. Repeat this layering format, saving just enough cheese slices to top off your tamale bowl. Once you have exhausted all of your ingredients, let the tamale rest for an hour, then heat for 3 minutes and enjoy!

SWEET AND SPICY CORNBREAD TAMALES

Ingredients:

4 – nice-size pieces of cornbread (on a day cornbread is served)

1 – sausage

1 – hot cheese bar

1 – bag of rice

1 – banana (optional)

10 – butter pats

6 – tablespoons of sugar

1 – chili seasoning pack

1 – big chip bag

chopped jalapeños

garlic powder

The Whip-Game:

Cut up your sausage into nice-sized squares. Cut your cheese bar into 32 slices. Chop up your jalapeños. Put your sausage and jalapeños in a bowl and cook for 1 minute. Save your banana until the rice is done. Crumble your cornbread so that there are no lumps. In another bowl, add in your rice and enough water to cover. To your cornbread, add all of the following: 6 tablespoons of sugar, chili seasoning pack, and 8 butter pats. Add warm water slowly while mixing with one hand. It should be somewhat tight; don't add too much water. At this point, use both hands and work the dough until you can make a ball, then let your dough rest. To your rice, add in your onion powder, half of your banana, and 2 butter pats, mix well. Take your chip bag and cut it down the center. Split your dough in half and take one ball and spread it on your chip bag, flattening it into a square and making sure you are able to fold in all 4 sides. After that, lay down 8 slices of cheese; top that with 1/2 of your rice, and then 1/2 of your meat and jalapeños, followed by 8 more cheese slices. Take the other 1/2 of the banana, slice it, and place it on top of your cheese. Use the bag to help you fold in the opposite sides one at a time, then fold in the ends, to make the tamale square. Repeat the same steps in making your other tamale. Enjoy. I love these different styles of tamales.

GUMBO, SOUP, PASTA, AND DUMPLINGS

ALL MEAT AND CHEESE SPICY GUMBO

Ingredients:

1 – summer sausage

1 – chicken pouch

1 – mackerel steaks

1 – beef stick

1 – hot cheese bar

1 – cheddar bar

1 – bottle of salsa

1 – bottle of hot sauce

12 – packs of ketchup

1/2 – bag of rice

onions (fresh if you can get them, if not substitute onion powder, garlic powder, and 2 Cajun shrimp seasoning packs from Ramen)

The Whip-Game:

Add just enough water to cover your 1/2 bag of rice in a bowl. Add 1 season pack mix and let it fluff up. Next, pour your whole bottle of salsa into a big bowl and add to it 1/2 a bottle of hot sauce and 12 packs of ketchup. Pour in one 8-ounce cup of hot water and boil for 4 minutes. In the water, place your cut-up sausage and chopped beef stick, chicken, and drained mackerel. Let this come to room temperature; Boil another 6-ounce cup of water. To your meat and sauce, add in your onions, if you have any. If not, add in your seasons, leaving the last Cajun shrimp pack out. Pour in your cup of hot water, and then quickly add your rice and the last seasoning pack. Gently stir. Just before you eat, take your cheese bars and cut them into big squares, placing as many as you would like in your bowl of one of Big Cal's favorites – from me to you.

SPICY NOODLE FISH SOUP

Ingredients:

2 – Ramen soups: hot and spicy or Cajun shrimp flavor

2 – packets of fish steaks with chili or mackerel

1 – serving of fresh lettuce (make on a day lettuce is served)

3 – butter pats.

The Whip-Game:

Place your whole Ramen soup in hot water, just to loosen it up. Once Ramen has separated, not to the point of puffing up, drain and add all 3 butter pats, then cook for 3 minutes, stopping after each minute to pull apart with a fork. Add in seasoning packs. In another bowl, boil about 12 ounces of water until it's boiling hot. To your cooked and seasoned Ramen, place 1/2 of your lettuce, and then add in 1 of your fish packs. On top of that, add in the rest of your lettuce and the other fish pack. Pour just enough boiling hot water to cover. You can eat this right away, while it's hot and ready. Enjoy this spicy and tasty soup.

HOT AND SPICY GARLIC CHUNKY CHICKEN SOUP

Ingredients:

2 – Ramen soups

1 – chicken pouch

3 – butter pats

1 – tablespoon of garlic powder

20 – ounces of water

The Whip-Game:

Take your chicken pouch and place it into a bowl, adding to it one of your hot and spicy seasoning packs with 1/2 of your garlic powder, and let it rest.

Place your 2 Ramen soups in boiling hot water – do not break them up, leave them whole. Let them sit in water long enough to come apart, but do not let them puff up. Place the Ramen in another bowl; add to that same water another 1/2 cup of water. Add in your other seasoning pack and the rest of the garlic and both butter pats, microwave for 1 minute and 30 seconds. Layer in your Ramen with your spicy chunky chicken in between. Reheat for 1 minute and enjoy this great-tasting soup.

SWEET AND SPICY PORK AND SAUSAGE SOUP

Ingredients:

2 – Ramen soups

1 – bag of pork rinds or skins.

1 – sausage log

2 – sweeteners or 3 tablespoons of granulated sugar

20 – ounces of water

The Whip-Game:

Cut up your sausage. To it, add 1/2 of the bag of pork rinds and 1 sugar pack. Cook in a microwave for 1 minute and 30 seconds. Place your 2 Ramen in boiling hot water; do not break them up, leave them whole. Let them sit in water long enough to come apart; do not let them puff up. Place Ramen in another bowl, add to that same water another 1/2 cup of water. Add in your other seasoning pack and the rest of the garlic and the sugar pack. Cook in a microwave for 1 minute and 30 seconds. Place into your hot seasoned water the Ramen soup, in layers, and in between each layer, your pork and sausage mixture. The very last thing is to add the other 1/2 of your pork rinds. Let your taste buds enjoy.

PIZZA PASTA – RANCH FLAVOR STYLE

Ingredients:

1 – box of macaroni and cheese

1 – pack of pepperoni

1 – sausage

1 – cheese bar

1 – pickle

3 – ranch salad dressing packs

1/2 – cup of jalapeños

onion and garlic powder

The Whip-Game:

Cut your sausage into small squares; cut your sliced pepperoni into nice-sized pieces. Cut your cheese bar into small squares and dice your pickle and jalapeños, saving 1/2 of the pickle juice. In a bowl, add your sausage and pepperoni. Cook for 1 minute. Boil six 8-ounce cups of water, and add 1 tablespoon of salt. When your water is boiling hot, add in the box of macaroni and stir. Then place back in the microwave and boil for 7 to 10 minutes until the macaroni is tender. Drain, add cold water, let sit for 50 seconds, then drain again. Add in your chopped pickle and jalapeños, and then stir in the pack of powder cheese and 1 tablespoon each of onion and garlic powder. Add in your sausage and pepperoni mixture and cheese bar. Add in all 3 packs of ranch salad dressing and stir well – let it sit until it becomes room temperature or sit it on ice. After eating such a dish, one will say, "squisito!" (delicious in Italian). Enjoy.

DUMPLINGS WITH SPICY CHICKEN.

Ingredients:

For dumplings:

1 – sleeve of Saltine crackers

1 – Ramen, chicken flavor

8 – butter pats

1 – tablespoon of salt

1 – 6-ounce cup of warm water

For spicy chicken:

1 – chicken pouch

1 – chicken seasoning pack

1 – quarter cup of chopped

8 – tablespoons of hot sauce

jalapeños and juice

onion and garlic powder

The Whip-Game:

Put chicken, jalapeños, and juice in a bowl to soak. Take your sleeve of saltines and crush them into a fine dust. Place dust in a big bag and add 6 pats of butter, 1 tablespoon each of salt and onion powder, and warm water slowly, stopping to mash saltine dust into a firm paste. When you can form a ball with the paste, it's done. Close the bag tightly. Place your chicken seasoning along with 1 tablespoon each of onion and garlic powder and 2 butter pats in a bowl. Add very hot water, just enough to stir and mix. Take your dumpling paste and roll up 12 to 16 dumplings. Coat them in the seasoning mix and add in your chicken, hot sauce, and the rest of the very hot water to where everything is covered.

Warm for 1 minute and 30 seconds, and enjoy these home-cooked dumplings.

BURRITOS

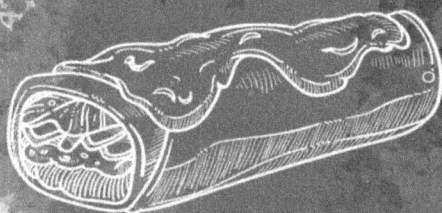

THE CALZILLÀ "BIG-BOY" BURRITO

Ingredients:

1 – pack of tortillas

1 – bag of rice

1 – squeeze cheese

1 – cheese bar

1 or 2 – summer sausages (1 pack of pepperoni, optional)

1 – chicken pouch

jalapeños

(you can also add honey, ranch dressing, bacon, etc., depending on your taste)

Other things needed: Newspaper and a piece of plastic big enough to wrap up six tortillas

The Whip-Game:

Slice summer sausage and cook for 2 minutes, 30 seconds. Add very hot water to the rice in a bowl, enough to cover. Don't cook the rice; just let it sit until it expands. Once the rice is done, season and add cheese. If you like, you can cook all of your other meats. Place the newspaper down with plastic on top, placing all six tortillas down to where they are overlapping each other: 3 at the top and 3 at the bottom. Paste them together with the squeeze cheese, then spread the cheese all over. If you are using pepperoni, place them down in the center, in rows of twos. You can then apply a layer of cheese rice on top. Then lay your diced bar of cheese, followed by your meat and jalapeños. Repeat laying layers until you are content, but please make sure you leave yourself room to wrap your Calzillà. Cook for 3 and 1/2 minutes or a total of 5 minutes, depending on the size.

TUCKED AND ROLLED CRUNCHY BURRITOS

Ingredients:

1 – pack of tortillas

1 – sausage or meat of choice

1 – bag of rice or 4 Ramen soups

1 – cheese bar or squeeze cheese

2 – bags of your favorite chips, crushed up

cheese

some kind of beans (optional)

honey and your favorite sauce

The Whip-Game:

Cook or fry your rice or Ramen, season it, and add jalapeños. Take your tortillas, place cheese down first, add beans and filling and meat, and place as many in your bowl. Next, add your sauce, topped off with some of your crushed chips. Tuck in the ends, slightly cover with honey, then roll them in the rest of your chips, and add extra sauce if wanted. Warm to your liking. Enjoy your tucked and rolled burritos.

CHEESE BBQ BURRITOS

Ingredients:

1 – pack of tortillas

1 – summer sausage

1 – bag of rice

1 – cheese bar

1 1/2 – cups of squeeze cheese

enough BBQ sauce to coat the meat

Onion powder and garlic powder

The Whip-Game:

In a bowl, add just enough water to cover your rice and let the rice fluff up. Then add in your 1.5 cups of squeeze cheese and a little seasoning.

Cut your sausage into six long strips and place them into a bowl. Season the sausage and cook it for 1 minute 30 seconds. Once it's cooked, coat the sausage strips with BBQ sauce and place them back into the microwave for another minute. Cut up your cheese bar also into long strips. Warm up your tortillas and make a bed in the center of each with some of your cheese rice. Place a strip of cheese followed by a strip of BBQ meat, and then top it off with another strip of cheese. If you like, add more sauce. Roll up these cheesy bad boys and enjoy.

PORK PARTY BURRITOS

Ingredients:

1 – 6-pack of tortillas

1 – pack of pepperoni

1 – pack of bacon

1 – bag of pork rinds or skins

1 – pork sausage

1 – bag of rice

1 – cheese bar /hot or cheddar

1 – pickle and onion powder

1/2 – cup, chopped

The Whip-Game:

Cut the sausage into nice-sized pieces. Cut the cheese bar into slices; try to cut 32 slices. In a bowl with your rice, add 1 and 1/2 tablespoons of onion powder, 1/2 bag of pork rinds, and 1/2 of your chopped jalapeños. Pour in enough water to cover. In another bowl, place your sausage, the rest of your jalapeños, and the other 1/2 bag of pork rinds. Cook for 1 minute, 30 seconds. Warm up your tortillas, placing them onto paper individually. Apply a large amount of rice to each one and add 5 slices of cheese to each one. Then lay 5 to 6 pepperoni slices, followed by applying your sausage mixture. Last, but not least, add a strip of bacon or bacon bits. Roll up your burritos, then wrap them tightly in paper. Heating time: 50 seconds to 1 minute. "Oink, Oink, baby!" Enjoy.

A BOWL BURRITO

Ingredients:

1 – single tortilla

1 – sausage log

1 – tablespoon of garlic powder

1 – butter pat

4 – tablespoons of salsa

1/2 – bag of rice

1/2 – cheese cup

The Whip-Game:

Cut up your sausage and cook it for 1 minute. To your rice, add your butter pat, 1 tablespoon of garlic powder, and just enough hot water to cover. Mix well and then stir in half of your cheese cup. Place your tortilla inside a cereal bowl. To it, add your rice and sausage, and then top it off with your 4 tablespoons of salsa and the rest of the cheese cup. Microwave for 1 minute and 30 seconds, and let it rest. Dig in and enjoy.

RICE DISHES

PORK OR BEEF FRIED RICE

Ingredients:

1 – bag of white or brown rice

1 – bag of pork rinds

1 – beef summer sausage or 1 – halal

1 – hot and spicy vegetable or beef seasoning pack from a Ramen

Make this meal on a day that mixed vegetables are served, get enough for 1 to 2 helpings.

The Whip-Game:

Take your rice and dry fry it until it's golden brown – anywhere between 2 to 3 minutes. Add just enough water to cover the rice and let it sit until it becomes fluffy. Cook your sausage for 2 minutes, add it to your fried fluffy rice, and stir in your mixed vegetables. If it's pork-fried rice, then just add your pork rinds; if it's beef-fried rice, just add in your meat. If you want beef-pork-fried rice, then add it all!

SPICY CHICKEN AND ORANGE FLAVORED RICE

Ingredients:

1 – chicken pouch

1 – bag of white rice

1 – hot and spicy season pack

1 or 2 oranges, only for zest and juices

chopped jalapeños to taste

The Whip-Game:

Place your chicken in a bowl. To it, add your hot and spicy seasoning pack, some of your chopped jalapeños, 2 butter pats, and cook with the lid on for 1 minute, 30 seconds. Let it rest. Take your oranges and cut each one into quarters, squeezing out juices and saving them to be used later. Remove the insides, including the white layer, leaving only the peel. Once this is done, take 4 of the peels, cut them into strips as thin as you can get them. Place the other 4 in a small bowl with just enough hot water to cover them. Let them sit for 15 more minutes, and then microwave for 50 seconds to 1 minute. Add this to your rice with enough water to cover. Add a pinch of salt. Once your rice has fluffed up, add in your thinly sliced orange peels and mix well. Add the squeezed orange juice to the chicken and reheat for 1 minute, and then pour it into your orange-flavored rice. Mix slightly. If you would like to add cheese, add in your favorite bar cheese, cut into small squares. This dish is so, so good. Enjoy with a bright orange smile.

MEAT DIRTY FRIED RICE

Ingredients:

3 – kinds of meat, including fish, your choice

1 – bag of rice.

1 – hot flavored Ramen

4 – butter pats

1 – quarter cup of chopped

2 – handful of peanuts or sunflower kernels

jalapeños to taste

The Whip-Game:

Cut up all meats into nice-sized chunks or squares; do not cut up fish if using. Take your rice and crushed up Ramen, placing the mixture into an empty popcorn bag. You are going to dry fry this mixture. Lay the bag flat in the microwave. Your first fry will be for 2 minutes. After 2 minutes, remove and shake. Place the bag back into the microwave and cook for another 3 to 4 minutes. Remove after each minute to shake. Do this until the mixture is golden brown. In another bowl, place all 4 butter pats, the hot and spicy seasoning pack, and 1 tablespoon each of onion and garlic powder. Pour golden brown dirty fried rice into a bowl with butter pats and seasoning, and shake to mix. Add just enough boiling hot water to cover. Take your meat, place it in a bowl, and add a handful of peanuts. Cook for 1 minute, 30 seconds. When done, pour into the rice mixture. Stir and mix well. Add in the other handful of nuts and chopped jalapeños. Reheat for 2 minutes. This dirty fried rice will have you cleaning your bowl. Enjoy another one of my favorite dishes.

FLUFFY JANE DOE RICE DISH

Ingredients:

1 – bag of rice

1 – mackerel or tuna pouch

1 – bag of sunflower kernels

1 – hot and spicy seasoning pack from Ramen

The Whip-Game:

Place your rice into a bowl, adding just enough water to cover. Once your rice is fluffy, add to it your fish, half a bag of sunflower kernels, and the hot and spicy seasoning pack. Mix in well. Then add the remaining sun kernels. If you would like to add cheese, use a cheese bar cut up into nice-sized squares. Once you eat this, Jane Doe, you can say you know who she is. Enjoy.

PUFFY JOHN DOE RICE DISH

Ingredients:

1 – bag of rice

1 – sausage log or beef stick

1 – chili seasoning pack from Ramen

1/2 – cup of salted peanuts

The Whip-Game:

Cut up your sausage log and cook for a minute. Place your rice into a bowl, adding just enough water to cover. Once your rice is puffed up, add to it your sausage, peanuts, and seasoning pack. Mix well. If you would like to add in some cheese, use a cheese bar cut up into nice-sized squares. This John Doe will be known. Enjoy.

SEAFOOD OCEAN BOWL

Ingredients:

1 – bag of rice

1 – mackerel or tuna pouch

1 – fish steaks and green chilies

1 – shrimp-flavored Ramen soup

The Whip-Game:

Place your rice into a bowl, adding just enough water to cover. Once your rice is fluffy, add to it all of your fish and the shrimp-flavored seasoning pack. Mix well. Enjoy the taste of the ocean.

MEXICAN STYLE FRIED RICE WITH SAUSAGE AND PEPPERONI

Ingredients:

1 – bag of rice

1 – sausage log

1 – bottle of salsa

1 – pack of pepperoni

2 – tablespoons of garlic

3 – tablespoons of honey

1 – diced pickle

3 – butter pats

1/2 – cup of chopped jalapeños

1/2 – cup of fresh onions chopped (if available, if not 2 tablespoons of onion powder)

The Whip-Game:

Cut up your sausage and pepperoni into nice-sized pieces. Cook together for 2 minutes. Fry your rice using the popcorn bag frying instructions. Once your rice is fried, add your whole bottle of salsa to it. Do not add water yet. Put in your butter pats. Now add your fresh onions, if available. If not, add in 1 tablespoon of onion powder and mix well. Now add just enough water to cover. Put in your meat mixture, jalapeños, and the rest of your onion and garlic powder. Cook for 3 minutes. When done, drizzle on your honey. Enjoy this very good style of rice.

CHEESE RICE AND POTATO CHIPS

Ingredients:

1 – bag of rice

1 – chili seasoning pack

2 – butter pats

2 – small bags (or 1 big bag) of your favorite chips, crushed

1/2 – bottle of squeeze cheese (or 1 nacho cheese cup)

The Whip-Game:

To your bag of rice, add just enough hot water to cover and set aside. Once it's done, add in your 2 butter pats and chili seasoning pack. Stir well. Take your crushed chips, using only half the bag, and mix them in. Then add in your cheese. Top off with the rest of your crushed chips. Enjoy this simple but good eat.

Calvin Brown

VARIETY OF RECIPES

CRUNCHY CRISPY FLAVOR BOWLS

Ingredients:

1 – pack of tortillas

1 – bag of rice

1 – cheese bar

1 – pickle

1 – bag of sunflower kernels

1 – ranch dressing

1 – chicken pouch

1 – sausage

1 – mackerel or pepperoni

1 – cereal bowl

The Whip-Game:

Slightly poke tortillas with a fork, wet with water, and then season. Turn the bowl upside down, place a tortilla on the inverted bowl, and microwave until the tortilla forms to the bowl. Remove and place the tortilla inside the bowl, right side up. Continue to cook until the tortilla becomes crispy and crunchy. Fill with cooked rice and add meat mixture, layering in whatever way you like, up to 4 or 5 layers. Once you have done your last layer, place your toppings: diced pickle, crumb cheese, sunflower kernels, and ranch dressing. You don't have to warm these delightful, crunchy, crispy bowls. But if you wish to, warm for 20 seconds, and enjoy these tasty, wonderful bowls.

MEATY CHILI MACARONI

Ingredients:

1 – box of macaroni and cheese

1 – sausage log

1 – beef stick

1 – chili pouch

2 – tablespoons each of garlic and onion powder

1/2 – cup of chopped jalapeño

1/2 – bottle of squeeze cheese

The Whip-Game:

Cut up your sausage log and beef stick. Add in your chicken pouch with 1 tablespoon of each onion and garlic powder. Cook for 2 minutes. Place macaroni into 6-8 ounces of boiling water, adding 1 teaspoon of salt. Boil for 7-10 minutes, until macaroni is tender. Drain, and then add in the cheese that comes with the macaroni. Add your meat mixture, chili seasoning pack, and 1/2 bottle of squeeze cheese chili pouch. To that, add the rest of your onion and garlic powder, and chopped jalapeños. Your chili macaroni is the "big macaroni." Enjoy.

DEEP DISH CHILI CHEESE FRITO BOWL WITH SPICY MEAT

Ingredients:

1 – big bag of Frito's

1 – chili pouch

1 – bottle of squeeze cheese

1 – sausage log

1 – chili seasoning pack

The Whip-Game:

Cut up your sausage into nice-sized squares, add in the seasoning pack, and cook for 1 minute, 30 seconds. Place your Fritos in a bowl and microwave for 2 minutes until you can smell them. Loosen up squeeze cheese by microwaving or adding water. You need to pour it. To your baked chips, pour on chili pouch and half of your squeeze cheese, mix them together well. Apply your chili-flavored sausage, topping it off with the rest of your cheese. Reheat for 1 minute, 30 seconds. Enjoy this bowl of fun.

LOCKED DOWN LASAGNA

Ingredients:

1 – pack of pepperoni

1 – bottle of squeeze cheese

1 – cheese bar

4 – Ramen soups

3 – packs of ranch salad dressing

2 – sausages

2 – tablespoons of garlic and onion powder

12 – slices of bread

18 – packs of mayo

1/2 – cup of chopped jalapeños

The Whip-Game:

Add just enough water to 6 slices of bread to make a ball of dough, and then add 1 tablespoon of each onion and garlic powder. Do this with the other 6 slices of bread. You will need two balls of seasoned dough. Cut up your sausage log into thin slices, and cook for 1 minute. Also, cut up your cheese bar into thin slices. Take your 3 packs of ranch salad dressing and mix them with your 18 packs of mayo. Stir well. Place your 4 Ramen soups in a bowl whole, do not break. Add water long enough to loosen. Press your seasoned dough ball into the bottom of your bowl, coming up the side of the bowl about an inch and a half. On top of the dough, apply some squeeze cheese, sliced pepperoni, and 2 of your Ramen layers, and season with 1 Ramen seasoning pack. Next, lay down a layer of meat and cheese bar, followed by applying half of your ranch and mayo mixture. Cover by flattening your second dough ball, and repeat these steps. Cook for 7-10 minutes, and then enjoy this Locked Down Lasagna.

CHEESE BUTTER GARLIC BREAD

Ingredients:

1 – cheese cup

4 – tablespoons of garlic powder

4-6 – slices of bread

4-6 – butter pats

The Whip-Game:

Butter your slices of bread on one side and then apply some garlic. Microwave the bread until the butter has baked into it and the bread has become slightly hard (but not too hard). Then apply a thick layer of your cheese. Microwave again for 30 seconds. Esquisito!

PEANUT BUTTER FRIED RAMEN. WITH OR WITHOUT SPICY SAUSAGE

Ingredients:

2 – tablespoons of peanut butter

3 – chili-flavored Ramen soups

1 – sausage log

1 – cup of water

The Whip-Game:

Crush up your Ramen and fry them using the popcorn bag instructions. Mix your 2-tablespoon of peanut butter and 2 chili seasoning packs with 4 ounces of water. Stir to loosen the peanut butter. If you want sausage, add it to this mix. Once your Ramen is fried golden brown, pour it into a bowl while it's hot and fresh out of the microwave. Cook it again for another minute. This is a really quick dish to make.

NACHOS

Calvin Brown

Notes on Nachos!

When "chips" are mentioned, use one of these two: round tortillas or Doritos. To thicken your nachos, add 1/2 bag of rice. Cook and apply whenever necessary. Nachos can be made in a bowl or on a chip bag.

CHEESE PIZZA NACHO PLATTER

Ingredients:

1 – big bag of chips or 3 small bags

1 – cheese bar

1 – nacho cheese cup (or some squeeze cheese)

1 – quarter cup of pizza sauce

1 – tablespoon onion powder (or fresh onions, if available)

1 – big chip bag is needed

The Whip-Game:

Cut up your pepperoni into small pieces, and your cheese bar into small squares. Place 1/2 of your bottle of squeeze cheese (or nacho cheese cup) into a bowl and add your fresh onions (or a tablespoon of onion powder) and 7 tablespoons of water. Cook for 1 minute. Cut open your big chip bag or lay down a big piece of plastic. Space your chips out on the bag and apply 1/2 of your cut-up pepperonis, followed by 1/2 of your small cheese squares, 1/2 of your pizza sauce, 1/2 of your squeeze cheese, and your onions. Following this same format, make a second layer. Sit back and enjoy your pizza platter with a smile…enjoy.

CHILI CHEESE NACHOS

Ingredients:

1 – big bag of chips (or 3 small bags)

1 – chili pouch (with or without beans)

1 – quarter cup of squeeze cheese

1 – chili seasoning pack from Ramen

These can be made in a bowl or on a big chip bag

The Whip-Game:

Pour your chili into a bowl and add 10 tablespoons of water and 1/2 of your quarter cup of shredded cheese. Cook for 1 minute. Place your chips in your bowl or on a big chip bag. Pour on your chili and cheese mixture, followed by applying the rest of your squeeze cheese, and adding on your chili seasoning pack. Simple, but so good. Enjoy.

TUNA NACHOS

Ingredients:

1 – big bag of chips (or 3 small bags)

1 – cheese bar

1 – quarter cup of squeeze cheese

1 – pickle

1 – tablespoon of garlic powder

2 – tuna pouches

7-10 – packs of mayo

1 – tablespoon of onion powder (or fresh onions, if available)

The Whip-Game:

Cut up the cheese bar into small squares and dice your pickle. Place both your tuna pouches in a bowl and add your fresh onions, if you have them. If not, add in your tablespoon of onion powder and mix well. In a bowl, mix your squeeze cheese and 7 tablespoons of hot water, then heat it for 1 minute. Place a layer of chips in a bowl or on a big chip bag, and then layer on your cheese squares, followed by your tuna and pickle. Top with a pinch of garlic powder and 3 packs of mayo. Repeat this layering process until the layers are complete and you are out of ingredients. Enjoy.

PORK STYLE NACHOS

Ingredients:

1 – big bag of chips (or 2 small bags)

1 – pack of pepperoni

1 – pack of bacon or bacon bits

1 – bag of pork rinds or skins

1 – pork sausage

1 – cheese bar

1 – bottle squeeze cheese

1 – pickle

1 – tablespoon of onion powder

The Whip-Game:

Cut up your pepperoni into pieces using scissors. Cut your sausage into squares. Crush your pork skins and dice your pickle. Cut your cheese bar into small squares. Add 10 tablespoons of water to your squeeze cheese and cook for 1 minute. Place your sausage and pork skins in a bowl with some of your pickle and cook for 1 minute. Cut open a big chip bag and spread a layer of chips over it. Add a layer of pepperoni, followed by sausage, pork skin mixture, and then your cheese squares and diced pickle. Top with squeeze cheese and bacon strips broken into small pieces or bacon bits. Repeat this layering format, and then enjoy this pork feast.

JALAPEÑO RANCH CHICKEN NACHOS

Ingredients:

1 – big bag of chips (or 3 small bags)

1 – chicken pouch

1 – nacho cheese cup (or squeeze cheese)

2 – ranch salad dressing packs

1 – pickle

1 – quarter cup of chopped jalapeños

1 – chicken seasoning pack from Ramen mixed with onion powder

The Whip-Game:

Dice your pickles and jalapeños. In a bowl, add your chicken, 1 ranch salad dressing pack, chicken seasoning, onion powder, diced pickle, and 1/2 of your chopped jalapeños. Mix well. In another bowl, add your squeeze cheese or nacho cheese cup and 7-10 tablespoons of water. Cook for 1 minute. In a bowl or on a big chip bag, place 1/2 of your chips and cover them with 1/2 of your squeeze cheese, followed by your chicken. Top it with 1/2 of your diced pickle and chopped jalapeños, and then add a ranch salad dressing pack. Follow this same format in layering your second layer, topping off with squeeze cheese and ranch salad dressing. Enjoy these mouthwatering chicken and ranch nachos. Smile while eating.

NACHO BELGRÁNDE

Ingredients:

2 – cheese bars

1 – chili pouch

2 – chicken pouches

2 – bags of refried beans and rice

1 – bottle of squeeze cheese

1 – pickle diced

1 – tablespoon of fresh onion, diced (or onion powder)

3 – ranch salad dressing packs

3 – bags of chips (1 large, 2 small)

1 – jar of bacon bits

1/2 – jar of chopped jalapeños

The Whip-Game:

This will feed up to a group of 5. Cut pepperoni into small pieces using scissors. Cut both sausages into cubes. Cut both cheese bars into small squares. Crush pork skins into pieces. In a microwavable bowl, combine your sausage, some of your pickle and jalapeño mixture, fresh onions (or a tablespoon of onion powder), and cook for 1 minute and 30 seconds. Next, place your beans and rice in a bowl and add enough water to cover. Add some of your squeeze cheese to your chili, cook for 1 minute, and stir well. Layout 2 big chip bags, cut open, as surface cover. Layout 1/2 of your chips, then layer on 1/2 of your cheese bars, 1 chicken pouch, 1/2 of your beans and rice, pepperonis, bacon bites, pickle, and jalapeños. Top with 1/2 of your chili and squeeze cheese mixture, and your sausage mixture. Use the rest of your ingredients for the second layer. Enjoy this nacho delicacy.

SNACKS

CHUNKY ROASTED BEAN DIP

Ingredients:

1 – bag of refried beans

1 – sausage

1 – pickle

3 – butter pats

1 – cup of squeeze cheese

3 – mustard packs

chopped jalapeños

The Whip-Game:

Cook your beans in a bowl for 1 minute, 30 seconds, until you smell them roasting. Add enough water to cover the beans, stir in your 3 butter pats. Cut your sausage and pickle into chunks; cook the sausage for 1 minute. Add the juice from your pickle to your beans, along with all 3 packs of mustard. Mix well, and then add in your sausage and pickle chunks. Your dip should be tight but somewhat loose. If not, add tablespoons of warm water to loosen. Warm for 30 seconds, and then add your cheese and jalapeños. Get a big bag of your favorite chips and start dipping. Enjoy.

GOOD MORNING GOODNESS

Ingredients:

1 – bag of white rice

1 – bag of trail mix or mixed nuts

1 – package of syrup

2 – butter pats

2 – tablespoons of sugar

The Whip-Game:

Take your rice, place it in a bowl, and your 2 butter pats, add in your sugar and just enough water to cover, let it sit until it becomes fluffy. Once your rice is done, add in your trail mix, mix everything together, and pour on your syrup. This morning, goodness will give you some energy that will start up your morning and last throughout your day. Enjoy.

HAND-2-MOUTH SNACK

Ingredients:

1 – bag of your favorite peanuts

2 – packs of flavored oatmeal

1 – pack or bag of M&Ms

1 – pack of your favorite cookies, broken into pieces

2 – cereal bars, broken into pieces

The Whip-Game:

After breaking the cookies and cereal bars into pieces, put all of your ingredients in a bag or bowl with a lid and shake vigorously to mix. Sit it on the desk in your room. Afterwards, every time you are in your bunk, you'll find yourselves putting your hand to your mouth, enjoying this right-on-time snack. Enjoy.

POTATO-CHIP INFUSION

Ingredients:

1 – jar of honey

1-or-2 – bags of microwave popcorn

4-to-5 – bags of your favorite chips

The Whip-Game:

You'll need a big bag, bowl, or clean foot basin. Pop both bags of popcorn, then mix them in a big bag with your chips. Shake to mix and then drizzle honey over this potato chip infusion. Sit back and enjoy this sweet, salty, and spicy explosion.

CHEESE COOKIE POPCORN CRUNCH BOWL

Ingredients:

1 – bag of microwave popcorn

1 – pack of chocolate chip cookies, broken into pieces

2 – small bags of Cheetos (or 1 big bag)

3 – butter pats

The Whip-Game:

Pop the popcorn and pour it into a big bowl or big bag. Add chocolate chip cookie pieces and your chips. Melt your butter and pour it onto the mixture. Shake the bag vigorously and enjoy.

DUMP TRUCK CHIP BAG

Ingredients:

1 – bag of corn chips

1 – sausage

1 – cheese bar diced

1 – pack of ranch salad dressing

1/2 – cup of squeeze cheese

The Whip-Game:

Cut up your sausage and cook for 1 minute and 30 seconds. Dice the cheese bar and mix your squeeze cheese and ranch dressing together. Take half of your chips out of their bag and add half of your other ingredients. Shake well. Put the unmixed chips back in the bag and cover with the remainder of your ingredients: Sit back and enjoy the dump truck.

STRAWBERRY AND CHOCOLATE HONEY BUN TOWER

Ingredients:

2 – honey buns

2 – strawberry bars

1 – pack of Oreo cookies

4 – tablespoons of hot chocolate mix

4 – tablespoons of strawberry jelly

2 – tablespoons of peanut butter

The Whip-Game:

Take your Oreos and break them into nice-sized pieces. Apply a tablespoon of peanut butter to both of your honey buns. Place a strawberry bar on top of that and add 2 tablespoons of hot chocolate mix. Pour on half of your Oreos, followed by 2 tablespoons of strawberry jelly. Stack the honey buns and apply the last of your ingredients on top. Microwave for 30 seconds, and then take your time while eating. Enjoy.

GO NUTS SNACK

Ingredients:

1 – pack of sunflower kernels

1 – pack of peanuts

2 – packs of corn-nuts, ranch, and Chile picante flavors

1 – bag of cashews

3 – tablespoons of honey

The Whip-Game:

Mix all the nuts in a bowl and shake well to mix. Top with honey and microwave for 50 seconds to 1 minute and 30 seconds. Shake until cooled down, and then *go nuts* eating this nutty snack.

CHOCOLATE STUFFED GRAHAM CRACKERS SANDWICHES

Ingredients:

1 – box of graham crackers

1 – box of dunking sticks (or Swiss rolls)

1 – pack of Oreo cookies

3 – tablespoons of peanut butter

4 – tablespoons of hot cocoa mix

8 – tablespoons of water

The Whip-Game:

Break your dunking sticks or Swiss rolls into chunks in a bowl. Add 3 tablespoons of peanut butter and 4 tablespoons of hot cocoa and mix well. Add in water and mix again. It should be thick. Then break your Oreos into pieces and add them by slightly folding them in. When this is done, start making your stuffed graham crackers sandwiches. You can also heat this for 20 seconds to add a little warmth. Enjoy this delight.

CAL'S MORNING HAPPINESS BOWL

Ingredients:

2 – packs of cinnamon oatmeal, any flavor

1 – sausage log

2 – tablespoons of sugar

1/2 – bag of peanuts

1/2 – bag of rice

The Whip-Game:

Put your rice in a bowl and add just enough water to cover. Cut your sausage log into nice-sized pieces and cook them for 1 minute, 30 seconds. Pour the juices from your sausage into your rice and add your 2 tablespoons of sugar, 1/2 bag of peanuts, and 2 packs of oatmeal. Top with your sausage pieces and mix slightly. Reheat for 30 seconds. I like this bowl because it has meat and oatmeal, which are two of my favorite things to eat. I truly hope you enjoy this as much as I do.

CHOCOLATE-COVERED BACON

Ingredients:

4 – packs of bacon (24 slices)

4 – Hershey's candy bars

1 – cut open chip bag

The Whip-Game:

Pull your bacon slices apart and cook them until they are crispy. Place on a paper towel or a piece of paper to suck up some of the oils. Once well dried, place them on a cut-open chip bag. Take a big mug or bowl, fill it with water, and bring it to a boil in the microwave. Place your candy bars, in their wrappers, into the water. Once they have melted, cut off one of the corners and coat your bacon strips on both sides. Cover with chocolate until your heart is content.

Ghetto Chips

There are many different ways these can be made and various flavors that can be produced. The flavor is strictly up to you. If you follow my "Whip-Game," you will come out on top, enjoying these self-made chips.

SPICY CHILI AND PEANUT BUTTER FLAVORED

Ingredients:

2 – Tablespoons of peanut butter

1/4 – cup of chopped jalapeños

3-to-4 – Ramen, spicy or chilled flavored

3-to-5 – butters pats

The Whip-Game:

Break your Ramen into bite-size pieces and place them in a bowl, and cover with cold water. Drain right away, add the seasoning pack, and shake to mix. Then microwave for 1 minute. Add in butter and jalapeños and microwave for 2 minutes, removing halfway through to shake and make sure the butter has coated all of the chips. Do this until your jalapeños are slightly fried. Last step, add in your peanut butter and cook for another 3 to 4 minutes, taking out after each minute to shake up until dark, crispy, and crunchy. They should look like little fried chicken wings. Warning: Keep your fingers out of the way when eating this bite-size wonder. Enjoy.

HONEY BBQ CHEESE FLAVORED

Ingredients:

5 – butters pats

3 – tablespoons of honey

1/4 – cup of BBQ sauce.

1/4 – cup of squeeze cheese

3-to-4 – Ramen soups, any flavor

The Whip-Game:

Break your Ramen into bite-size pieces and place them in a bowl, and cover with cold water. Drain right away. If you choose, you can add 1 seasoning pack from Ramen. Add in 3 of your 5 butters, and microwave for 2 minutes, removing halfway through to shake and make sure the butter has coated all of the chips. Cook until golden brown, and then apply some honey and the last 2 butters. Microwave for 30 seconds and then pour on your BBQ sauce. Shake to coat the chips and then microwave for another minute and a half. At this stage, apply your cheese and the rest of your honey. Cook until your BBQ sauce and cheese look like it has been baked on and your chips are crunchy to your liking. Remember – look out for your fingers when eating these bite-size wonders. Enjoy.

SWEET AND SPICY CHEESE FLAVORED

Ingredients:

7 – butter pats

4 – tablespoons of granulated sugar (or 4 sweeteners)

1 – quarter cup of squeeze cheese

3-to-4 – Ramen, hot and spicy or chili flavored soups

The Whip-Game:

Break Ramen soups into nice-sized pieces. Place them in a bowl and cover with cold water. Drain right away. Add 4 butter pats and cook for 1 minute, 30 seconds. Mix 3 of your seasoning packs with 3 tablespoons of sugar and pour the mixture onto the Ramen soups. Shake to coat. Cook for 2 minutes. After each minute, pull out and shake. Mix your cheese and your last spoonful of sugar with 4 tablespoons of water. Stir until loose and pour onto the chips. Cook for another 2 minutes, pulling out to shake. Cook until your chips are crunchy and golden-colored. Please look out for your fingers. Enjoy.

CRISPY SPICY PORK-CHOP FLAVORED

Ingredients:

1 – tablespoon of onion powder

2 – chili seasoning packs

8 – butter pats

1/2 – bottle of hot sauce

4-to-6 – Ramen soups

The Whip-Game:

Mix your 1/2 a bottle of hot sauce, 1 chili seasoning pack, and 2 butter pats. Cook for 50 seconds. Break your Ramen soups into nice-sized pieces in a bowl and cover with cold water. Drain immediately and top with 4 butter pats. Cook for 1 minute, 30 seconds. Mix 1 of your seasoning packs with 1 tablespoon of onion powder, sprinkle on Ramen soups, and shake to coat. Cook for 2 minutes, shaking after each minute. After 2 minutes, add some of your hot sauce mixture and cook for another 3-4 minutes, pulling out the bowl and shaking after each minute. Just before the last minute, add in your last 2 butters and the rest of your hot sauce mixture. Cook until crunchy and golden in color. Please look out for your fingers, once again. Enjoy.

HONEY GARLIC SPICY BBQ FLAVORED

Ingredients:

1 – quarter cup of BBQ sauce

2 – tablespoons of garlic powder

7 – tablespoons of hot sauce

7 – butter pats

15 – tablespoons of honey

4-to-5 – hot and spicy Ramen soups

The Whip-Game:

Mix your honey and 1 tablespoon of garlic powder. Thoroughly stir 3 hot seasoning packs into your BBQ sauce. In a bowl, break your Ramen soups into nice-sized pieces. Cover with cold water and drain right away. Add 1 seasoning pack from Ramen, 3 of your butter pats, and your hot sauce. Cook in a microwave for 2 minutes. After each minute, remove from the microwave and shake to make sure every chip is coated. Cook until golden brown. Then apply some of your honey and garlic powder mixture and the last 4 butters. Microwave for 30 seconds and then pour on your BBQ sauce. Shake to coat the chips. Microwave for another minute and a half. At this stage, cook until your BBQ sauce and honey until it looks like it has been baked on, and your chips are crunchy to your liking. Remember … try not to bite your fingers.

CHEESE RANCH AND BACON FLAVORED

Ingredients:

1 – pack of bacon, chopped or in bits

1 – tablespoon of garlic powder

2 – packs of ranch salad dressings

6 – butter pats

4-to-5 – Ramen soups

The Whip-Game:

Mix your squeeze cheese and 1 pack of ranch salad dressing. In a bowl, break your Ramen into nice-sized pieces and cover with cold water. Drain right away and add 4 butter pats. Cook for 1 minute, 30 seconds. Add 3 of your seasoning packs to 1 tablespoon of garlic powder, mix, and put on your Ramen soups. Shake to coat. Cook for 2 minutes. After each minute, pull out and shake. Pour your cheese and ranch mixture onto the chips and cook for another 3-4 minutes. Pull out to shake after each minute. In your last minute, add on your last ranch salad dressing pack and 2 butters, and add bacon. Cook until baked. Don't eat your fingers; you are going to need them. Enjoy.

HONEY MUSTARD AND JALAPEÑO FLAVORED

Ingredients:

1 – handful of chopped jalapeños and juice

8 – mustard packages

6 – butter pats

2 – sweeteners

12 – tablespoons of honey

4-to-5 – Ramen soups

The Whip-Game:

Thoroughly mix your mustard packages, 6 tablespoons of honey, both sweeteners, and jalapeño juice. Break your Ramen into nice-size pieces, placing them in a bowl, and cover with cold water. Drain right away and add the seasoning pack. Shake to mix, then microwave for 1 minute. Add in 6 butters and 1/2 of the honey and jalapeño mixture. Place back into the microwave for 2 minutes. After 1 minute, take out and shake well to make sure the butter and honey mixture has coated all of the chips. Do this until your jalapeños are slightly fried. The last step is to add the last 6 tablespoons of honey and cook for another 3-4 minutes. Take out after each minute and shake up until dark, crispy, and crunchy. Warning: Eat with caution. Enjoy.

BEVERAGES

LEMON PEPPERMINT SWEET TEA

Ingredients:

1 – bag of instant sweet tea

1 – bag of lemon Kool-Aid

1 – bag of peppermints (or 3 sticks), crushed up

7 – tablespoons of sugar

7-to-10 – tablespoons of honey

The Whip-Game:

Makes 2 quarts; Boil four 8-ounce cups of water for a full 2 minutes. Add to it your crushed-up mint candies and sugar. Let this mixture chill for half an hour. Add three 8-ounce cups of warm water to your whole bag of instant tea and stir until the sugar is no longer visible. Mix by stirring your mint candy, and place it in the microwave for another minute and a half. Continue stirring until the candies have turned into a liquid. Combine the candy mix with the tea mix and stir in your honey. Let this mixture chill for a full hour. When it's time, pour over ice and enjoy this refreshing tea.

ORANGE CINNAMON SUMMER ICED TEA

Ingredients:

1 – bag of orange breakfast mix or orange Kool-Aid

1 – orange

1 – bag of atomic fireballs

8 – ounces of granulated sugar (or 15 sweetener packs)

10 – tea bags

The Whip-Game:

Bring four 8-ounce cups of water to a boil. Crush your atomic fire balls, add them, your orange drink mix, and sugar to your boiling water. Stir until the ingredients have turned into liquid, and then set aside. Heat another four 8-ounce cups of water for 3 minutes. Cut your orange into quarters and squeeze out the juices. Pour some of your hot water onto your orange slices, just enough to draw out the juices. Add your 10 tea bags to the rest of your hot water and let them sit for 45 minutes. Mix in the juices from your orange slices with your tea, and then mix that with the Fireball and orange drink mixture. Let it chill until you're ready to have a taste of the summer. Enjoy.

FANTASTIC FRUITY COOLER

Ingredients:

1 – packet of every flavor of Kool-Aid on your canteen

1 – white soda (like Sprite or Sierra Mist)

1 – pack of Gatorade

The Whip-Game:

Mix 6 tablespoons of each flavor of Kool-Aid available to you, or 1 of every kind of Cool-Off mix drink you can find, or mix them both together in a large container or Kool-Aid picture with the water recommended. Pour in half of your white soda and stir until all the ingredients have turned into liquid. Pour in your pack of Gatorade and the rest of your soda. Place some crushed ice in your cup. Drink and cool off. Enjoy.

BUSTIN' LEMON AND FRUIT PUNCH ICED TEA

Ingredients:

1 – box of tea

1 – bag of lemonade (or sugar-free lemonade)

1 – box of sugar-free fruit punch

1 – bag of fruit punch Kool-Aid

1 – Sprite or Sierra Mist soda

5 – single tea bags

The Whip-Game:

Place your 5 tea bags into 20 ounces of boiling-hot water. If you are using sugar-free Kool-Aid, then take 5 single packs of lemonade flavor and 5 single packs of fruit punch flavor and pour them into your pitcher with half of your soda. When done brewing, add your tea to your pitcher and stir in the rest of your soda. Let cool, then pour into a big cup of ice. Enjoy this bustin' flavorful drink.

RISE UP AND GO DRINK

Ingredients:

1 – Sierra Mist or Sprite

4 – tea bags

4 – sugar sweeteners

5 – tablespoons of sugar

8 – tablespoons of orange breakfast mix (or 2 sugar-free packs)

The Whip-Game:

Pour half of your soda into a large cup and stir in your orange breakfast mix. Microwave until this mixture is boiling, add your tea bags, and let steep for 2 minutes. After brewing, remove the tea bags and add your sugar. Stir thoroughly and then pour in the rest of your soda. Fill your pitcher halfway with ice and pour in your "rise up" drink. Now, pour yourself a cup, and go get your day rolling!

PEPPERMINT ICED COFFEE

Ingredients:

5 – peppermint candies (or 1 stick), crushed up

4 – tablespoons of sugar

3 – tablespoons of creamer

2 – tablespoons of coffee

The Whip-Game:

Place your crushed-up mints in a cup of hot water and microwave for 1 minute. Add your sugar and creamer. Stir and then add your coffee. Let cool, and then add ice. Now enjoy that minty kick!

CHOCOLATE PEPPERMINT ICE COFFEE

Ingredients:

4 – tablespoons of hot chocolate

3 – peppermint candies, crushed up

4 – tablespoons of sugar

3 – tablespoons of creamer

2 – tablespoons of coffee

The Whip-Game:

Place your crushed-up mints in a cup of hot water and microwave for 1 minute. Add your sugar and creamer. Stir and then add your coffee and hot chocolate. Let cool, and then add ice. Now enjoy that minty chocolate kick!

CREAMY BUTTERSCOTCH COFFEE – HOT

Ingredients:

4 – butterscotch candies, crushed up

4 – tablespoons of sugar

3 – tablespoons of creamer

2 – tablespoons of coffee

The Whip-Game:

Place your crushed-up candies in a cup of hot water and microwave for 1 minute. Add sugar and creamer. Stir well, and then add in your coffee. Add in 2 more tablespoons of creamer and reheat to your liking.

I am very picky when it comes to eating something somebody else has cooked.

The following section is occupied by those I've tipped my cook's hat to. What I've tasted from these brothers brought a smile to my taste buds. That's why I'm sharing their goodness with you. The cooks mentioned have given me, Calvin Brown, their consent to place their very own recipes in my cookbook. I give special thanks to them all.

BONUS RECIPES

LITTLE BIG MAN'S FAMOUS CHILI CHEESE BAKED CORN CHIPS

Ingredients:

1 – big bag of corn chips (or 3 small bags)

1 – chili seasoning pack from a Ramen soup

1 – pouch of chili without beans

1/2 – a bottle of squeeze cheese

The Whip-Game:

Pour your corn chips into a popcorn bag. Next, add just enough very hot water to your squeeze cheese to loosen it so it can be applied smoothly (you can also microwave it). Place your popcorn bag into the microwave for 3 to 4 minutes, taking it out to shake after every minute. The corn chips should smell like you have baked them, and their color should be a darker, golden brown. Once you have gotten them to this point and they are hot, pour them into a bowl, and apply your squeeze cheese. Cover with enough to coat them well, and then shake the bowl to set the cheese. Reheat them in the microwave for 2 minutes, or until they seem to be baked. After that, sprinkle on your seasoning pack. Make sure that you have something to clean off your hands and fingers, because these cheese-baked corn chips can become sticky, and they are finger-licking good! Enjoy.

BOZEY GEE'S SWEET PIMPIN' PEANUT BUTTER POPCORN

Ingredients:

1 – butter pat

2 – bags of popcorn

3 – tablespoons of peanut butter

3 – sugar sweeteners

The Whip-Game:

Pop your popcorn and pour it into a big bag or bowl. In a separate bowl, add your butter, peanut butter, and sweeteners, and microwave for 1 minute. Stir until it's creamy, and pour this mixture on your popcorn. Shake well. This sweet-and-salty mixture tastes just like pimpin' at its best. Enjoy this one-of-a-kind treat.

BILLIONAIRE CANNON'S BANANA PUDDING

Ingredients:

1 – pack of coffee creamer

1 – cup of pudding

1 – pack of cookies (chocolate chip, vanilla wafers, or duplex)

6 – tablespoons of sugar

3 – butter pats

3 – tablespoons of honey

2 – granola bars, your choice

4 – bananas

The Whip-Game:

In a bowl, mix creamer, sugar, 2 butter pats, a pudding cup, and 1 banana until creamy. Layer the bottom of the bowl with cookies. Chop 1 and 1/2 bananas into rounds and cover the entire cookie layer. Next, pour your mixture evenly over this layer of cookies and bananas. Complete 2-4 layers, depending on the depth of your bowl. When you have completed the layering of your choosing, take the remaining cookies (about 10) and crush them, add 1 butter pat, and mix together like a crumble. When the cookie crumble is ready, apply it evenly to the top layer of pudding. Crush your 2 granola bars over the cookie crumble, and then drizzle with honey in a side-to-side motion. Chill on ice until cold. This delight is one that I truly enjoy every time I have it. Thank you, Mr. Cannon.

SMOOTH AZZ B-J'S CHICKEN SALAD WITH OR WITHOUT PORK SKINS

Ingredients:

1 – box of macaroni

1 – cheese bar

1 – tablespoon of onion powder

1 – chicken seasoning pack from a Ramen soup

1 – bag of pork skins

2 – butter pats

10 – packs of mayo

1-2 – chicken pouches

1/2 – cup of jalapeños, chopped

The Whip-Game:

Cut up your cheese bar into nice-sized squares. Crush up your pork skins. Pour six 8-ounce cups of water into a bowl, add 1 tablespoon of salt, and boil for 3 minutes. Then add in your macaroni, stir, and cook in the microwave for another 7-10 minutes, until the macaroni is tender. Drain and add cold water, covering the macaroni for 50 seconds, then drain again. Add your 2 butter pats, the powder cheese, your chopped jalapeños, and chicken seasoning pack. Add a tablespoon of onion powder to your precooked chicken pouches, mix, and then add it into your macaroni, along with your cheese bar and 7-10 mayo packs. Mix to a creamy texture. If you desire pork skins, add them now as a topping. This chicken salad can be enjoyed warm or cold. Either way, it's creamy and delightful. Enjoy.

Calvin Brown

WRAPS, MELTS, TACOS & QUESADILLAS

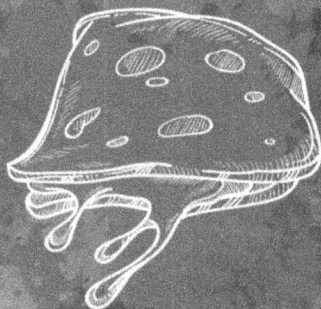

RANCH AND BACON WRAPS

Ingredients:

1 – pack of tortillas

1 – tablespoon of onion powder

1 – tablespoon of garlic powder

2 – packs of bacon

2 – cheese bars

2 – packs of ranch salad dressing

1/2 – bag of rice

The Whip-Game:

Cut your cheese bars into nice-sized slices. In a bowl, put your 1/2 bag of rice and add just enough hot water to cover. Once cooked, add your onion and garlic powder, and 1 pack of ranch salad dressing. Stir well. To each tortilla, add a small amount of rice, a layer of cheese, two slices of bacon, and top with ranch salad dressing. Roll them up and enjoy.

RAMEN AND FISH STEAKS WRAPS

Ingredients:

3 – shrimp or hot and spicy flavored Ramen soups

2 – fish steaks pouches

2 – butter pats

1/2 – jalapeño, chopped

The Whip-Game:

Crush Ramen and cook using the popcorn bag frying instructions. Then place in a bowl and add just enough water to cover the noodles, 2 butter pats, and 2 seasoning packs. Place your fish steaks in another bowl, add your 1/2 cup of chopped jalapeños, and the last seasoning pack. Warm your tortillas, place a small bed of ramen on each, then top with your fish. Wrap them up and enjoy.

SAUSAGE AND TUNA CHEESE MELTS

Ingredients:

1 – pack of tortillas

1 – bag of rice

1 – sausage

1 – tuna pouch

1 – pickle, diced

2 – cheese bars

1 – jalapeño, diced

1 – bottle of squeeze cheese

1 – container of onion powder (or plain onions)

The Whip-Game:

Slice your sausage vertically and season with onion powder. Cook for 1 minute. Cook your rice, either by the instructions on the bag, or fry it, your choice. After your rice is done, mix in some of your diced pickle and jalapeño. Fold into your sausage your tuna and mix well. Season with just a little bit more onion powder, but do not cook it. Cut your 2 cheese bars into squares, put in a bowl, and add water or milk, just under a quarter cup. Microwave until it is melted and loose. Layer into your tortillas your rice mix, topped with your sausage and tuna. If you have fresh onions, place some on next (or sprinkle with onion powder) and then pour on your cheese, coating everything heavily. If you have honey or some kind of dressing, add that after you warm up your cheese melts for 20 seconds. Set back and be melted away. Enjoy.

SPICY SOFT COLD TUNA TACOS

Ingredients:

1 – 6-pack of tortillas

4 – Ramen soups, hot or Cajun

2 – tuna pouches

1 – bar of cheddar cheese, hot

1 – pickle

4 – butter pats

2 – tablespoons of onion powder

honey to taste

The Whip-Game:

Cut your cheese bars into nice-sized slices. Dice your pickle and crush all 4 Ramen soups. Place your crushed Ramen in a big bowl with all of the butter pats, 3 seasoning packs, 1 tablespoon of onion powder, and just enough hot water to cover everything. Microwave for 3 minutes and 30 seconds. Let it cool down completely. Another bowl season your tuna pouches with your last pack of seasoning, onion powder, and 1/2 of your diced pickle. Stir. Layer each of your tortillas with 4 to 6 slices of cheese, cooked Ramen, another 4 to 6 slices of cheese, your tuna mixture, and top with 1 tablespoon of honey. Enjoy these great tuna tacos.

Calvin Brown

SPICY CHEESE QUESADILLAS

Ingredients:

1 – 6-pack of tortillas

2 – cheese bars

1/2 – cup of jalapeño slices

The Whip-Game:

Cut your cheese bars into thin slices. Place 5 to 6 slices on each tortilla and top with jalapeños slices. Fold and microwave until cheese is melted. Enjoy.

CHEESE ROASTED BEAN QUESADILLAS

Ingredients:

1 – 6-pack of tortillas

4 – butter pats

1 – cheese bar

1 – bag of beans

1/4 – cup of squeeze cheese

1 1/2 – tablespoons of onion powder

(If you would like to add meat to these, just follow my "Chunky Roasted Bean Dip Recipe.")

The Whip-Game:

Place your beans in an empty popcorn bag and cook in the microwave for 1 minute, 30 seconds, until you smell them roasting. Pour them into a bowl, add butter pats, onion powder, and enough hot water to cover. Add a cup of squeeze cheese and stir well. Warm tortillas add beans and cheese, fold, and enjoy. If these are not enough for you, have you a bag of chips with them. Enjoy.

CASSEROLES

DELUXE GUMMY CHEESE RAMEN CASSEROLE

Ingredients:

4 – Ramen soups

1 – sausage log

1 – chicken pouch

1 – bag of your favorite chips, crushed

1/2 – bag of rice

1/2 – bottle of squeeze cheese

The Whip-Game:

Cut your sausage log into slices and cook for 1 minute. Mix in your chicken pouch and 2 seasoning packs and cover with a lid. Crush your 4 Ramen soups and place them in another bowl with your 1/2 bag of rice. Add just enough hot water to cover and cook for 2 minutes. Add in your sausage and chicken mixture, and 1/2 of your bottle of squeeze cheese. Mix well, microwave for a minute, then add in your crushed chips. This gummy cheese casserole will fill you up. Enjoy.

CRAZY DEEP-SEA CASSEROLE

Ingredients:

2 – Ramen soups, shrimp-flavored

1 – bag of rice

1 – tuna pouch

2 – mackerel pouches

1 – nacho cheese cup

3 – packs of mayo

2 – tablespoons of onion powder

2 – pats of butter

The Whip-Game:

In your first bowl, cook your rice. Once your rice is done, add 1/2 of your cheese cup and stir well. Crush your Ramen in another bowl. Add 1 tablespoon of onion powder, 2 butter pats, and just enough hot water to cover. Pour mackerel into another bowl and mash into a paste using a fork. Add 1 shrimp seasoning pack and 1 tablespoon of onion powder. In a fourth bowl, mix your tuna pouch and 3 mayo packs. At the bottom of your fifth bowl, spread a nice layer of rice, using 1/2 from the first bowl. On top of that, add 1/2 of your seasoned mackerel, then your Ramen, a layer of tuna, the other 1/2 of your rice, mackerel again, and tuna again. Top by spreading evenly the rest of your cheese in the cup. If you want to, you can add some sliced jalapeños. Microwave for 2 minutes and 30 seconds. Another one that the people love and enjoy.

THE ALL-IN GOLDEN BOWL

Ingredients:

1 – bag of rice

1 – pack of bacon

1 – sausage log

1 – cheese bar

1 – bottle of salsa

1/2 – cup of chopped jalapeños

The Whip-Game:

This dish is truly an "all-in," just like an outstanding poker hand. Cut your sausage log into big pieces and your cheese bar into nice pieces. Microwave your bacon until it's crispy, then break it into pieces. Place all of your ingredients in your bowl, add enough water to cover, and then microwave for 4-5 minutes. If you would like to add some squeeze cheese on top, or your favorite sauce, go ahead – go all-in and enjoy.

BIG CALS
COMISSARY DELIGHTS

After eating one of Big Cal's 5-star meals, you may have room for a slice of mouth-watering, mind-blowing, heart-stopping, mouth-dropping delights.

The cakes, cheesecakes, and other delights in this section have given many taste buds an everlasting joy!

PIE CRUST

In many of these recipes, you will be instructed to make a "crust." Here's how it's done:

The Whip-Game:

Crush one pack of cookies (the type of cookies will depend on the recipe) into a fine powder. Add 4 tablespoons of sugar and 3 butter pats. Then add 8 tablespoons of water. If you want a chocolate- or peanut butter-flavored crust, add 3 tablespoons of cocoa or 1 tablespoon of peanut butter. Mix all of these ingredients together until you are able to form a ball of dough. Knead your dough into a flat-bottom bowl, pressing it evenly up the sides of the bowl, about an inch and a half high all around. Cook for 2 minutes, and it will puff up. When you remove it from the microwave, take a spoon and re-flatten your crust. Let it rest before adding your filling.

CAKES & PIES

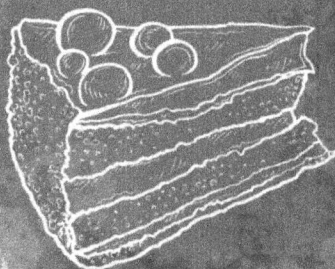

TWO-TIER CHOCOLATE CAKE WITH LEMON FROSTING AND CARAMEL GLAZING

Ingredients:

1 – white soda

2 – packs of sandwich cookies, duplex or chocolate flavored

6 – vanilla caramels (or 10 tablespoons of vanilla cappuccino)

12 – butter pats

14 – tablespoons of sugar

1/2 – bag of coffee creamer

1/4 – cup of lemon Kool-Aid (or 1 sugar-free pack of lemonade)

The Whip-Game:

Take cookies and remove the cream to use later. Crush both packs of cookies individually. In a bowl, mix 1 pack of cookies, 6 tablespoons of sugar, 3 tablespoons of coffee creamer, and 4 butter pats. Slowly pour in 1/2 of your white soda while stirring. The mixture should not be too wet and loose. Cook in the microwave for 3-5 minutes. It will puff. Pull out and check for wet spots. When there are no wet spots, put it under a fan to cool or just let it sit out. Once it has cooled, flip it onto a flat lid or piece of cardboard. Repeat the same steps for the second layer.

For the frosting and glazing, pour the bag of creamer into a bowl, adding the remaining sugar, lemon Kool-Aid, and 6 butter pats. Pour in a small amount of water, stirring to blend in. Mix well. Add water as you go. The frosting should be fluffy and thick. Spread an even layer of lemon frosting between the layers. With the rest of the frosting, cover the whole cake. Let it rest before you apply your glazing. If you don't have vanilla caramel, use vanilla cappuccino. Take 10 tablespoons of cappuccino, adding to it 2 butter pats, 3 tablespoons of sugar, and 6 tablespoons of water.

Microwave for 1 to 2 minutes until it thickens, and then glaze the top of the 2-tier cake.

TWO-TIER LEMON RED LICORICE CAKE WITH LEMON FROSTING

Ingredients:

1 – white soda

1 – Kool-Aid (or 1 sugar-free pack)

1 – pack of red licorice cut into small pieces

6 – vanilla caramels (or 10 tablespoons of vanilla cappuccino)

2 – packs of sandwich cookies, any flavor

10 – butter pats

14 – tablespoons of sugar

1/2 – bag of coffee creamer

1/4 – cup of lemonade

The Whip-Game:

Take cookies and remove the cream to use later.

Crush both packs of cookies individually. In a bowl, mix 1 pack of cookies, 6 tablespoons of sugar, 3 tablespoons of coffee creamer, and 4 butter pats. Slowly pour in 1/2 of your white soda while stirring. The mixture should not be too wet and loose. Cook in a microwave for 3-5 minutes. It will puff up. Pull out and check for wet spots. When there are no wet spots, put it under a fan to cool or just let it sit out. Once it has cooled, flip it onto a flat lid or piece of cardboard. Repeat the same steps for the second layer.

For the frosting, take your bag of creamer and pour it into a bowl. Add the remaining sugar, lemon Kool-Aid, and 6 butter pats. Pour a small amount of water, stirring to blend in, and mix well. Add water as you go. Your frosting should be fluffy and thick. Spread an even layer of lemon frosting between your layers and add some of your red licorice pieces. With the rest of the frosting, cover the whole cake. Let it rest before you apply the remainder of your red licorice pieces. Let it rest again. Then enjoy.

STRAWBERRY WITH A PEANUT BUTTER FROSTING

Ingredients:

1 – white soda

2 – packs of sandwich cookies, any flavor

2 – tablespoons of peanut butter

4 – strawberry bars

6 – vanilla caramels (or 10 tablespoons of vanilla cappuccino)

10 – butter pats

14 – tablespoons of sugar

1/2 – bag of coffee creamer

1/2 – cup of crushed peanuts

The Whip-Game:

Take cookies and remove the cream to use later.

Crush both packs of cookies individually. Place 1 pack of cookies in a bowl and add 2 strawberry bars. Add 6 tablespoons of sugar, 3 tablespoons of coffee creamer, and 4 butter pats. Slowly pour in 1/2 of the white soda while stirring. The mixture should not be too wet and loose. Cook in the microwave for 3-5 minutes. It will puff up. Pull out and check for wet spots. When there are no wet spots, put it under a fan to cool or just let it sit out. Once it has cooled, flip it onto a flat lid or piece of cardboard. Repeat the same steps for the second layer.

For the frosting, pour the bag of creamer into a bowl. Add the remaining sugar and 6 butter pats. Pour a small amount of water, stirring to blend in, and mix well. Add water as you go. The frosting should be fluffy and thick. Spread an even layer of peanut butter frosting between the layers. Top with peanuts. With the rest of the frosting, cover the whole cake. Let it rest before you apply the remainder of the peanuts. Let it rest again. Then enjoy.

PEANUT BUTTER WITH CHOCOLATE AND CAPPUCCINO FROSTING

Ingredients:

1 – white soda

2 – packs of sandwich cookies, any flavor

3 – tablespoons of cocoa mix

4 – tablespoons of peanut butter

6 – vanilla caramels (or 10 tablespoons of vanilla cappuccino)

6 – butter pats

12 – tablespoons of cappuccino

14 – tablespoons of sugar

1/2 – bag of coffee creamer

The Whip-Game:

Take cookies and remove the cream to use later. Crush both packs of cookies individually. In a bowl, mix 1 pack of cookies, 2 tablespoons of peanut butter, 6 tablespoons of sugar, 3 tablespoons of coffee creamer, and 2 butter pats. Add 2 butter pats, and slowly pour in 1/2 of the white soda while stirring. The mixture should not be too wet and loose. Cook in a microwave for 3-5 minutes. It will puff up. Pull out and check for wet spots. When there are no wet spots, put it under a fan to cool or just let it sit out. Once it has cooled, flip it onto a flat lid or piece of cardboard. Repeat the same steps for the second layer.

For the frosting, pour the bag of creamer into a bowl. Add the remaining sugar, 2 butter pats, 2 tablespoons of peanut butter, 3 tablespoons of cocoa mix, and 2 tablespoons of cappuccino. Pour in a small amount of water, stirring to blend. Mix well. Add water as you go. The frosting should be fluffy and thick. Spread an even layer of frosting between the layers. Frost the entire cake with the remainder of the frosting. Let it rest before applying the caramel glazing. Let it rest again. Then enjoy.

RED VELVET WITH CHOCOLATE AND PEANUT BUTTER FROSTING

Ingredients:

1 – white soda

2 – packs of sandwich cookies, any flavor

8 – butter pats

3 – tablespoons of cocoa mix

2 – tablespoons of red Kool-Aid (or 1 sugar-free pack)

4 – tablespoons of peanut butter

6 – vanilla caramels (or 10 tablespoons of vanilla cappuccino)

14 – tablespoons of sugar

1/2 – bag of coffee creamer

The Whip-Game:

Take cookies and remove the cream to use later. Crush both packs of cookies individually. In a bowl, mix 1 pack of cookies, 2 tablespoons of red Kool-Aid or sugar-free packet, 6 tablespoons of sugar, 3 tablespoons of coffee creamer, and 4 butter pats. Slowly pour in 1/2 of the white soda while stirring. The mixture should not be too wet and loose. Cook in the microwave for 3-5 minutes. It will puff up. Pull out and check for wet spots. When there are no wet spots, put it under a fan to cool or just let it sit out. Once it has cooled, flip it onto a flat lid or piece of cardboard. Repeat the same steps for the second layer.

For the frosting, pour the bag of creamer into a bowl. Add the remaining sugar, 4 butter pats, 2 tablespoons of peanut butter, and 3 tablespoons of cocoa mix. Pour a small amount of water, stirring to blend in, and mix well. Add water as you go. The frosting should be fluffy and thick. Spread an even layer of frosting between the layers. Frost the entire cake with the remainder of the frosting. Let it rest before applying the caramel glazing. Let it rest again. Then enjoy.

BANANA WITH PEANUT BUTTER FROSTING

Ingredients:

1 – white soda

2 – packs of sandwich cookies, any flavor

8 – butter pats

1 – banana cut in half

4 – tablespoons of peanut butter

6 – vanilla caramels (or 10 tablespoons of vanilla cappuccino)

14 – tablespoons of sugar

1/2 – bag of coffee creamer

The Whip-Game:

Take cookies and remove the cream to use later. Crush both packs of cookies individually. In a bowl, mix 1 pack of cookies, half of a banana, 6 tablespoons of sugar, 3 tablespoons of coffee creamer, and 4 butter pats. Slowly pour in 1/2 of your white soda while stirring. The mixture should not be too wet and loose. Cook in the microwave for 3-5 minutes. It will puff up. Pull out and check for wet spots. When there are no wet spots, put it under a fan to cool or just let it sit out. Once it has cooled, flip it onto a flat lid or piece of cardboard. Repeat the same steps for the second layer.

For the frosting, pour the bag of creamer into a bowl. Add the remaining sugar, 4 butter pats, and 2 tablespoons of peanut butter. Pour in a small amount of water, stirring to blend in. Mix well. Add water as you go. The frosting should be fluffy and thick. Spread an even layer of frosting between the layers. Frost the entire cake with the remainder of the frosting. Let it rest before applying the caramel glazing. Let it rest again. Then enjoy.

STRAWBERRY OREO CHEESECAKE

Ingredients:

1 – pack of Oreos without cookie filling (14-ounce or more)

1 – 1/2 strawberry bar (or strawberry wafers)

1 – bag of coffee creamer

6 – tablespoons of sugar

8 – butter pats

1/2 – bag of instant milk

The Whip-Game:

See directions on pie crust at the beginning of this "Commissary Delights" section, then proceed to make your filling as follows:

In a bowl, mix the bag of creamer, 1/2 bag of instant milk, 6 tablespoons of sugar, and 8 butter pats in a bowl. Add 10 tablespoons of cold water while stirring. Add water when needed. Stir until all ingredients are smooth and mixed together.

Add 1/2 strawberry bar or strawberry wafers and 1/2 pack of Oreos, saving the rest for your toppings. Pour the filling onto the crust. Let it settle, then add the toppings. If you want to add caramel for topping, make your own by using the caramel recipe in this book. Enjoy this delight.

LEMON CARAMEL PEPPERMINT CHEESECAKE

Ingredients:

1 – pack of cookies without cookie filling (14-ounce or more)

1 – bag of coffee creamer

6 – tablespoons of sugar

8 – butter pats

6 – tablespoons of lemon Kool-Aid (or 1 sugar-free pack)

1 – stick (or 8 pieces) peppermint, crushed

1/2 – bag of instant milk

caramel – use the "homemade caramel" recipe

The Whip-Game:

See directions on pie crust at the beginning of this "Commissary Delights" section, then proceed to make your filling as follows:

In a bowl, mix the bag of creamer, 1/2 bag of instant milk, 6 tablespoons of sugar, and 8 butter pats in a bowl. Microwave peppermints and 8 tablespoons of water until they become a liquid. Mix with other ingredients. Stir until smooth and mixed together. Pour the filling into the crust. Let it settle, then add toppings. If you want to add caramel for topping, make your own by using the caramel recipe in this book. Enjoy this delight.

PEANUT BUTTER OREO CHEESECAKE

Ingredients:

1 – bag of coffee creamer

6 – tablespoons of sugar

4 – butter pats

2 – tablespoons of peanut butter

2 – packs of Oreos

1/2 – bag of instant milk

The Whip-Game:

See directions on pie crust at the beginning of this "Commissary Delights" section, then proceed to make your filling as follows:

In a bowl, mix the bag of creamer, 1/2 bag of instant milk, 6 tablespoons of sugar, and 4 butter pats. Add 2 tablespoons of peanut butter and 1 pack of Oreos. Add 10 tablespoons of cold water while stirring. Add water when needed. Stir until all ingredients are smooth and mixed together. Pour filling into the crust. Let it settle, then top with the other pack of Oreos. If you want to add caramel for topping, make your own by using the caramel recipe in this book. Enjoy this delight.

PEANUT BUTTER SWISS ROLL CHEESECAKE

Ingredients:

1 – pack of cookies without cookie filling (14-ounce or more)

1 – bag of coffee creamer

3 – tablespoons of peanut butter

4 – Swiss rolls

1/2 – bag of instant milk

12 – tablespoons of sugar

10 – butter pats

The Whip-Game:

See directions on pie crust at the beginning of this "Commissary Delights" section, then proceed to make your filling as follows:

In a bowl, mix the bag of creamer, 1/2 bag of instant milk, 6 tablespoons of sugar, and 4 butter pats. Add 2 tablespoons of peanut butter and 2 Swiss rolls. Add 10 tablespoons of cold water while stirring. Add water when needed. Stir until all ingredients are smooth and mixed together. Pour the filling into the crust and let it settle. Add the remaining 2 Swiss rolls, cut into small slices, as a topping. If you want to add caramel for topping, make your own by using the caramel recipe in this book. Enjoy this delight.

FREELAND'S CHUNKY DELUXE CHEESECAKE

Ingredients:

1 – pack of cookies without cookie filling (14-ounce or more)

1 – bag of coffee creamer

6 – tablespoons of sugar

4 – butter pats

2 – tablespoons of peanut butter

2 – packs of Oreos

1 – Snickers bar cut into chunks

1 – pack of peanut M&M's

1 – Reese's Peanut Butter Cup

1/2 – bag of instant milk

The Whip-Game:

See directions on pie crust at the beginning of this "Commissary Delights" section, then proceed to make your filling as follows:

In a bowl, mix the bag of creamer, 1/2 bag of instant milk, 6 tablespoons of sugar, 4 butter pats. Add 2 tablespoons of peanut butter and 1 pack of Oreos. Add 10 tablespoons of cold water while stirring. Add water when needed. Stir until all ingredients are smooth and mixed together. Add in all the cut-up candy bars and M&M's. Pour the filling into the crust. Let it settle, then add the remaining pack of Oreos for your topping. If you want to add caramel for topping, make your own by using the caramel recipe in this book. Enjoy this delight.

STRAWBERRY CARAMEL CHEESECAKE

Ingredients:

1 – bag of coffee creamer

6 – tablespoons of sugar

8 – butter pats

3 – strawberry bars or wafers

1/2 – bag of instant milk

The Whip-Game:

See directions on pie crust at the beginning of this "Commissary Delights" section, then proceed to make your filling as follows:

Mix the bag of creamer, 1/2 bag of instant milk, 6 tablespoons of sugar, and 8 butter pats in a bowl. Add 10 tablespoons of cold water while stirring. Add water when needed. Stir until all ingredients are smooth and mixed together. Then add in 2 strawberry bars or strawberry wafers. Pour the filling into the crust. Let it settle, then add on the caramel and last strawberry bar or wafers for topping. If you want to add caramel for topping, make your own by using the caramel recipe in this book. Enjoy this Delight.

ROOT BEER FLOAT CHEESECAKE

Ingredients:

1 – pack of cookies without cookie filling (14-ounce or more)

1 – bag of coffee creamer

6 – tablespoons of sugar

8 – butter pats

1/2 – bag of instant milk

8 to 10 – pieces of root beer candies, crushed

caramel – from recipe in that section

The Whip-Game:

See directions on pie crust at the beginning of this "Commissary Delights" section, then proceed to make your filling as follows:

Mix a bag of creamer, 1/2 bag of instant milk, 6 tablespoons of sugar, and 8 butter pats in a bowl. Microwave root beer candies and 8 tablespoons of water until they become a liquid. Mix with other ingredients. Stir until smooth and mixed together. Pour the filling into the crust. Let it settle, then add on your toppings. If you want to add caramel for a topping, make your own by using the caramel recipe in this book. Enjoy this delight.

CHOCOLATE PEANUT BUTTER CRUNCH PIE

Ingredients:

1 – jar of peanut butter

1 – pack of cookies

1 – Hersey candy bar

7 – tablespoons of hot cocoa

3 – handfuls of peanuts

10 – tablespoons of sugar

1/2 – bag of cereal (Rice Krispies or Cornflakes)

The Whip-Game:

See directions on pie crust at the beginning of this "Commissary Delights" section, then proceed to make your filling as follows:

Mix together 1/2 jar of peanut butter, 10 tablespoons of sugar, and 7 tablespoons of cocoa. Microwave for 50 seconds to soften the peanut butter. Mix well. Mix 1/2 bag of cereal and a handful of peanuts and cookie pieces. Fold this mixture, trying not to crush up the cereal. Pour this mixture into the crust. Break candy bar into pieces. Microwave candy bar pieces, 8 tablespoons of water, and 2 butter pats for 50 seconds until it has melted. Pour it on top of the crunch pie and add a handful of peanuts. Enjoy.

OREO SNICKERS CRUNCH PIE

Ingredients:

1 – jar of peanut butter

1 – pack of cookies

1 – pack of Oreos

1 – Snickers

3 – handfuls of peanuts

7 – tablespoons of hot cocoa

10 – tablespoons of sugar

1/2 – bag of cereal (Rice Krispies or Cornflakes)

The Whip-Game:

See directions on pie crust at the beginning of this "Commissary Delights" section, then proceed to make your filling as follows:

Mix together 1/2 jar of peanut butter, 10 tablespoons of sugar, and 7 tablespoons of cocoa. Microwave for 50 seconds to soften the peanut butter. Mix well. Mix 1/2 bag of cereal, a handful of peanuts, and 1/2 pack of Oreos and cookie pieces. Fold in this mixture, trying not to crush up the cereal. Pour this mixture into the crust. Break candy bar into pieces. In a cup, microwave candy bar pieces, 8 tablespoons of water, and 2 butter pats for 50 seconds until it has melted. Pour it on top of the crunch pie. Top with a handful of peanuts and the remaining crushed Oreos. Enjoy.

MILKY WAY OATMEAL PIE.

Ingredients:

1 – jar of peanut butter

1 – pack of cookies

7 – tablespoons of hot cocoa

3 – handfuls of peanuts

2 – Milky Way candy bars

2 – packs of flavored oatmeal

10 – tablespoons of sugar

1/2 – bag of cereal (Rice Krispies or Cornflakes)

The Whip-Game:

See directions on pie crust at the beginning of this "Commissary Delights" section, then proceed to make your filling as follows:

Mix together 1/2 jar of peanut butter, 10 tablespoons of sugar, and 7 tablespoons of cocoa. Microwave for 50 seconds to soften the peanut butter. Mix well. Mix 1/2 bag of cereal, a handful of peanuts, 2 packs of oatmeal, and 1 Milky Way and cookie pieces. Fold in this mixture, trying not to crush up the cereal. Pour the mixture into the crust. Break candy bar into pieces. Microwave candy bar pieces, 8 tablespoons of water, and 2 butter pats in a cup for 50 seconds until it has melted. Pour it on top of the crunch pie. Top with a handful of peanuts. Enjoy.

BIG CAL'S MUD PIE

Ingredients:

1 – pack of sandwich cookies

1 – box of brownies

1 – bag of peanuts

1 – pack of Oreo cookies

6 – tablespoons of cappuccino

2 – butter pats

The Whip-Game:

See directions on pie crust at the beginning of this "Commissary Delights" section, then proceed to make your filling as follows: In a bowl, break brownies into big pieces, add 2 tablespoons of cappuccino, and 8 tablespoons of water. Heat in the microwave until the mixture becomes creamy. Mix in half of your peanuts and pour this on top of your crust. Evenly top with Oreo cookies after breaking them into pieces, then add a layer of peanuts. Next, use the recipe in this book for caramel sauce. Drizzle the caramel on top. Note: if you don't have brownies, use Swiss rolls. This is one of the most requested, no joke. So, truly enjoy this.

PEANUT BUTTER AND CHOCOLATE PIE

Ingredients:

1 – bag of creamer

1 – bag of hot cocoa

8 – tablespoons of sugar

3 – tablespoons of peanut butter

3 – butter pats

2 – ounces of hot water

1/2 – cup (4 ounces) of peanuts

The Whip-Game:

Mix all the ingredients in a bowl, except for your 3 tablespoons of peanut butter and 1/2 cup of peanuts. Stir well. Microwave for 4 minutes, but do not allow it to boil over. Once the texture of the ingredients pulls together and is tight when stirring, add in your peanut butter and peanuts. Mix well. Let it rest in the bowl. You can place the bowl on a bed of ice to chill. Cut and enjoy.

Pie Crust:

Crush one pack of cookies (the type of cookies will depend on the recipe) into a fine powder. Add 4 tablespoons of sugar and 3 butter pats. Then add 8 tablespoons of water. If you want a chocolate- or peanut butter-flavored crust, add 3 tablespoons of cocoa or 1 tablespoon of peanut butter. Mix all of these ingredients together until you are able to form a ball of dough. Knead your dough into a flat-bottom bowl, pressing it evenly up the sides of the bowl, about an inch and a half high all around. Cook for 2 minutes, and it will puff up. When you remove it from the microwave, take a spoon and re-flatten your crust. Let it rest before adding your filling.

CINNAMON GRANOLA APPLE COBBLER

Ingredients:

1 – pack of cookies

6 – apples

4 – butter pats

2 – packs of oatmeal

3 – granola bars

12 – tablespoons of sugar

The Whip-Game:

Break your cookies into pieces and layer them across the bottom of your bowl. Peel and dice 6 apples, add 8 tablespoons of sugar, and 4 butter pats. Cook until it thickens, let cool, and then pour on top of the cookie crust. Mix 2 packs of cinnamon oatmeal and 4 tablespoons of sugar, and then pour on top of your apple mixture. Break your 3 granola bars into nice-sized pieces to top your apple cobbler. Enjoy this wonderful delight.

BROWNIES, BARS & CLUSTERS

REESE'S PEANUT BUTTER CUP BROWNIES

Ingredients:

1 – bag of hot cocoa

1 – pack of sandwich cookies, broken into big pieces

1 – pack of oatmeal

1 – Reese's Peanut Butter Cup

8 – tablespoons of sugar

5 – butter pats

2 – tablespoons of peanut butter

The Whip-Game:

In a bowl, mix your whole bag of cocoa, 8 tablespoons of sugar, 5 butter pats, and 16 tablespoons of water. Microwave for 3 minutes and 30 seconds. While this mixture is pulling together, stir in your cookie pieces, 2 tablespoons of peanut butter, and 1 pack of oatmeal. Mix well. Pour dough into a snack cracker box lined with a big chip bag. Break your candy bar into pieces and place in a cup with 8 tablespoons of water and 2 butter pats. Microwave for 50 seconds, or until it has melted into a liquid, and then pour it on top of your brownies. They are so good, you will think they came straight from George Washington Carver.

MILKY WAY BROWNIES

Ingredients:

1 – bag of hot cocoa

1 – pack of sandwich cookies, broken into big-size pieces

1 – pack of oatmeal

1 – Milky Way

8 – tablespoons of sugar

5 – butter pats

2 – tablespoons of peanut butter

The Whip-Game:

In a bowl, mix your whole bag of cocoa, 8 tablespoons of sugar, 5 butter pats, and 16 tablespoons of water. Microwave for 3 minutes and 30 seconds. While this mixture is pulling together, stir in your cookie pieces and 1 pack of oatmeal. Mix well. Pour dough into a snack cracker box lined with a big chip bag. Break your candy bar into pieces and place in a cup with 8 tablespoons of water and 2 butter pats. Microwave for 50 seconds, or until it has melted into a liquid, and then pour it on top of your brownies. They are so good you will think they came straight from the Mars chocolate factory.

SNICKERS AND CHICK-O-STICK BROWNIES

Ingredients:

1 – bag of hot cocoa

1 – pack of sandwich cookies, broken into big pieces

1 – pack of oatmeal

1 – Snickers

1 – Chick-O-Stick, crushed

8 – tablespoons of sugar

5 – butter pats

2 – tablespoons of peanut butter

The Whip-Game:

In a bowl, mix your whole bag of cocoa, 8 tablespoons of sugar, 5 butter pats, and 16 tablespoons of water. Microwave for 3 minutes and 30 seconds. While this mixture is pulling together, stir in your cookie pieces and 1 pack of oatmeal. Mix well. Pour dough into a snack cracker box lined with a big chip bag. Break your candy bar into pieces and place in a cup with 8 tablespoons of water and 2 butter pats. Microwave for 50 seconds, or until it has melted into a liquid, and then pour it on top of your brownies. Top with your crushed Chick-O-Stick. They are so good, you will think they came straight from Betty Crocker.

M&M PEANUT BROWNIES

Ingredients:

1 – bag of hot cocoa

1 – pack of sandwich cookies, broken into big size pieces

1 – pack of oatmeal

2 – tablespoons of peanut butter

2 – packs of M&M's peanut

8 – tablespoons of sugar

5 – butter pats

The Whip-Game:

In a bowl, mix your whole bag of cocoa, 8 tablespoons of sugar, 5 butter pats, and 16 tablespoons of water. Microwave for 3 minutes and 30 seconds. While this mixture is pulling together, stir in your cookie pieces, 1 pack of oatmeal, and 1 pack of M&M's. Mix well. Pour dough into a snack cracker box lined with a big chip bag. Top with your other bag of M&M's, crushed. Allow brownies to harden. They are so good, you will think they came from a store.

CRUNCH BERRY BROWNIES

Ingredients:

1 – bag of hot cocoa

1 – pack of sandwich cookies, broken into big pieces

1 – pack of oatmeal

1 – 8-ounce cup of Crunch Berry cereal

8 – tablespoons of sugar

5 – butter pats

2 – tablespoons of peanut butter

The Whip-Game:

In a bowl, mix your whole bag of cocoa, 8 tablespoons of sugar, 5 butter pats, and 16 tablespoons of water. Microwave for 3 minutes and 30 seconds. While this mixture is pulling together, stir in your cookie pieces, 1 pack of oatmeal, and 1 cup of Crunch Berry cereal. Mix well. Pour dough into a snack cracker box lined with a big chip bag. Allow to harden. They are so good, you will think they came from a bakery.

PEANUT BUTTER CARAMEL CLUSTERS

Ingredients:

1 – bag of coffee creamer

5 – butter pats

2 – tablespoons of peanut butter

5 – tablespoons of syrup

8 – tablespoons of hot cocoa

1 – bag of peanuts

14 – tablespoons of water

10 – tablespoons of sugar

1/2 – bag of cappuccino

The Whip-Game:

In a bowl, mix the bag of creamer, 1/2 bag of cappuccino, 10 tablespoons of sugar, 5 butter pats, 6-tablespoon of syrup, 8 tablespoons of cocoa, and 16 tablespoons of water. Stir to an even consistency. Microwave for 3 minutes and 30 seconds. Watch while cooking; do not let it boil over. Cook it until it pulls together while stirring. Once it gets to this point, mix in your bag of peanuts and peanut butter. Spread this mixture evenly onto a big chip bag. Forming dough into appropriate-size clusters. These will take care of your sweet tooth. Enjoy.

CHOCOLATE CARAMEL CLUSTERS

Ingredients:

1 – bag of coffee creamer

1 – bag of peanuts

1 – Snickers candy bar

5 – butter pats

8 – tablespoons of hot cocoa

10 – tablespoons of sugar

14 – tablespoons of water

1/2 – bag of cappuccino

The Whip-Game:

In a bowl, mix the bag of creamer, 1/2 bag of cappuccino, 10 tablespoons of sugar, 5 butter pats, 8 tablespoons of cocoa, 1 Snickers, and 16 tablespoons of water. Stir to an even consistency. Microwave for 3 minutes and 30 seconds. Watch while cooking; do not let it boil over. Cook it until it pulls together while stirring. Once it gets to this point, mix in your bag of peanuts. Spread this mixture evenly onto a big chip bag. Forming dough into appropriate-size clusters. These will take care of your sweet tooth. Enjoy.

CHOCOLATE PEANUT BUTTER OREO BARS

Ingredients:

1 – bag of coffee creamer

1 – bag of peanuts

1 – Snickers bar

2 – packs of Oreo's

5 – butter pats

2 – tablespoons of peanut butter

8 – tablespoons of hot cocoa

16 – tablespoons of water

10 – tablespoons of sugar

1/2 – bag of cappuccino

The Whip-Game:

In a bowl, mix the bag of creamer, 1/2 bag of cappuccino, 10 tablespoons of sugar, 5 butter pats, 8 tablespoons of cocoa, 1 Snickers, 1 pack of Oreo, and 16 tablespoons of water. Stir to an even consistency. Microwave for 3 minutes and 30 seconds. Watch while cooking; do not let it boil over. Cook it until it pulls together while stirring. Once it gets to this point, mix in the peanut butter, your bag of peanuts, and another pack of Oreos. Spread this mixture evenly onto a big chip bag. Cut the dough into appropriate-sized bars. These will take care of your sweet tooth. Enjoy.

NO-BAKE COOKIES

NO–BAKE PEANUT BUTTER COOKIES

Ingredients:

1 – Reese's Peanut Butter Cup

5 – tablespoons of peanut butter

2 – packs of oatmeal

1/2 – cup of hot cocoa

The Whip-Game:

Mix all the ingredients in a bowl until you reach a thick and even consistency. Form cookies from your no-bake cookie dough on a big chip bag. You should be able to form and make 12 to 16 cookies. They truly are delightful. Enjoy.

CHOCOLATE NO-BAKE COOKIES

Ingredients:

5 – tablespoons of peanut butter

2 – packs of oatmeal

1 – Hershey's candy bar

1/2 – cup of hot cocoa

The Whip-Game:

Mix all the ingredients in a bowl until you reach a thick and even consistency. Form cookies from your no-bake cookie dough on a big chip bag. You should be able to form and make 12 to 16 cookies. They truly are delightful. Enjoy.

NO-BAKE PEPPERMINT SNICKERS COOKIES

Ingredients:

5 – tablespoons of peanut butter

2 – packs of oatmeal

1 – Snickers candy bar, chopped into small pieces

2 – peppermint candies, crushed

1/2 – cup of hot cocoa

The Whip-Game:

Mix all the ingredients in a bowl until you reach a thick and even consistency. Form cookies from your no-bake cookie dough on a big chip bag. You should be able to form and make 12 to 16 cookies. They truly are delightful. Enjoy.

M&MS NO-BAKE COOKIES

Ingredients:

5 – tablespoons of peanut butter

2 – packs of oatmeal

1 – bag of M&Ms, crushed

1/2 – cup of hot cocoa

The Whip-Game:

Mix all the ingredients in a bowl until you reach a thick and even consistency. Form cookies from your no-bake cookie dough on a big chip bag. You should be able to form and make 12 to 16 cookies. They truly are delightful. Enjoy.

NO-BAKE OREO/CHICK-O-STICK COOKIES

Ingredients:

5 – tablespoons of peanut butter

2 – packs of oatmeal

1 – pack of Oreos

1 – Chick-O-Stick

1/2 – cup of hot cocoa

The Whip-Game:

Mix all the ingredients in a bowl until you reach a thick and even consistency. Form cookies from your no-bake cookie dough on a big chip bag. You should be able to form and make 12 to 16 cookies. They truly are delightful. Enjoy.

SWEET TAFFY

LEMON FLAVOR SWEET TAFFY

Ingredients:

1 – bag of creamer

3 – ounces of water

5 – butter pats

2 – ounces of sugar

1/2 – cup of Kool-Aid (or 2 sugar-free packs)

The Whip-Game:

If using regular Kool-Aid, mix all the ingredients in a bowl. If not, mix everything except the sugar-free Kool-Aid. Add 2 ounces of hot water and stir. Mix well and microwave for 4 minutes. Keep an eye on it, because it will boil over. Once the ingredients pull together and become tight while stirring, it's done (if you are using sugar-free Kool-Aid, stir it in now). Pour it onto a big chip bag that's been cut open and spread out.

GRAPE FLAVOR SWEET TAFFY

Ingredients:

1 – bag of creamer

3 – ounces of Kool-Aid (or 2 sugar-free packs)

5 – butter pats

2 – ounces of sugar

1/2 – cup water

The Whip-Game:

If using regular Kool-Aid, mix all the ingredients in a bowl. If not, mix everything except the sugar-free Kool-Aid. Add 2 ounces of hot water and stir. Mix well and microwave for 4 minutes. Keep an eye on it, because it will boil over. Once the ingredients pull together and become tight while stirring, it's done (If you are using sugar-free Kool-Aid, stir it in now). Pour it onto a big chip bag that's been cut open and spread out.

CHERRY FLAVOR SWEET TAFFY

Ingredients:

1 – bag of creamer

3 – ounces of Kool-Aid (or 2 sugar-free packs)

5 – butter pats

2 – ounces of sugar

1/2 – cup water

The Whip-Game:

If using regular Kool-Aid, mix all the ingredients in a bowl. If not, mix everything except the sugar-free Kool-Aid. Add 2 ounces of hot water and stir. Mix well and microwave for 4 minutes. Keep an eye on it, because it will boil over. Once the ingredients pull together and become tight while stirring, it's done (If you are using sugar-free Kool-Aid, stir it in now). Pour it onto a big chip bag that's been cut open and spread out.

ORANGE FLAVOR SWEET TAFFY

Ingredients:

1 – bag of creamer

3 – ounces of Kool-Aid (or 2 sugar-free packs)

5 – butter pats

2 – ounces of sugar

1/2 – cup water

The Whip-Game:

If using regular Kool-Aid, mix all the ingredients in a bowl. If not, mix everything except the sugar-free Kool-Aid. Add 2 ounces of hot water and stir. Mix well and microwave for 4 minutes. Keep an eye on it, because it will boil over. Once the ingredients pull together and become tight while stirring, it's done (If you are using sugar-free Kool-Aid, stir it in now). Pour it onto a big chip bag that's been cut open and spread out.

FRUIT PUNCH FLAVOR SWEET TAFFY

Ingredients:

1 – bag of creamer

3 – ounces of Kool-Aid (or 2 sugar-free packs)

5 – butter pats

2 – ounces of sugar

1/2 – cup water

The Whip-Game:

If using regular Kool-Aid, mix all the ingredients in a bowl. If not, mix everything except the sugar-free Kool-Aid. Add 2 ounces of hot water and stir. Mix well and microwave for 4 minutes. Keep an eye on it, because it will boil over. Once the ingredients pull together and become tight while stirring, it's done (If you are using sugar-free Kool-Aid, stir it in now). Pour it onto a big chip bag that's been cut open and spread out.

CHOCOLATE FLAVOR SWEET TAFFY

Ingredients:

1 – bag of creamer

3 – ounces of hot cocoa

5 – butter pats

2 – ounces of sugar

1/2 – cup of water

The Whip-Game:

Mix all the ingredients in a bowl. Add 2 ounces of hot water and stir. Mix well and microwave for 4 minutes. Keep an eye on it, because it will boil over. Once the ingredients pull together and become tight while stirring, it's done. Pour it onto a big chip bag that's been cut open and spread out.

SAUCES, CARAMEL & FROSTING

SPICY MAPLE HONEY MUSTARD

Ingredients:

2 – hot and spicy Ramen seasoning packs

2 – packs of maple syrup

6 – tablespoons of honey

24 – packs of mustard

The Whip-Game:

Place all of the ingredients in a bowl and stir until it is mixed well and smooth. Store in a bottle; it will not go bad.

HONEY GARLIC BUTTER

Ingredients:

3 – tablespoons of garlic powder

6 – tablespoons of honey

2 – tablespoons of sugar

12-to-16 – butter pats

The Whip-Game:

Melt your butter pats in the microwave and then add your garlic powder and sugar. Stir until the butter has cooled down and takes a form. Store in a container or bowl with a lid.

SWEET AND SPICY BBQ SAUCE

Ingredients:

1 – hot and spicy seasoning pack

24 – packs of ketchup

1/2 – bottle of white soda

1/2 – bottle of hot sauce

6 – tablespoons of sugar

The Whip-Game:

Place all of the ingredients into a bowl and cook until it thickens. Stir until cool and then place in a bottle.

HOMEMADE PIZZA/BBQ SAUCE

Ingredients:

1 – bottle of salsa

2 – tablespoons of onion powder

2 – tablespoons of garlic powder

1 – bottle of white soda

12 – packs of ketchup

1/2 – bottle of hot sauce

The Whip-Game:

Place all of the ingredients into a bowl and cook until it thickens. Stir to cool down and then place in a bottle.

SPICY AND SWEET PEANUT BUTTER SAUCE

Ingredients:

4 – tablespoons of peanut butter

2 – chili seasoning packs

3 – tablespoons of sugar (or 3 sweeteners)

5 – tablespoons of jalapeño juice

12 – tablespoons of warm water

The Whip-Game:

Place 3 of your 4 tablespoons of peanut butter in a bowl. Add 6 tablespoons of warm water, 1 chili seasoning pack, and 2 tablespoons of sugar (or 2 packs of sweetener) and stir until all is mixed well. Microwave for 30 seconds, and then add the rest of your ingredients. Stir until loose and pliable. If you need to thin the sauce, add more jalapeño juice and not water. This sauce is good on any kind of pork dish. Enjoy.

HOMEMADE CARAMEL WITH CAPPUCCINO

Ingredients:

3 – butter pats

5 – tablespoons of sugar

8 – tablespoons of creamer

10 – tablespoons of water

10 – tablespoons of cappuccino

The Whip-Game:

Mix all of the ingredients in a big bowl and stir well. Microwave for 3 minutes, or until it thickens and pulls together when stirring. This will make enough to cover a 2-tier cake.

BASIC INGREDIENTS FOR FROSTING

Ingredients:

6 – tablespoons of sugar

6 – butter pats

1 – pack any flavor Kool-Aid

12 – tablespoons of water (you may add more water if needed)

1/2 – bag of creamer

The Whip-Game:

Mix all ingredients together and stir until fluffy and thick.

A Special Thanks

Every word that is written on this page came from wlthin my cooking soul and is extended to both of my families: biological and prison. I would like to say "thank you" to all who know me and have written reviews on my cooking. I would also like to say thanks for all of your inspiration, it helped push me to open up and share my love for cooking with the world. Not only that, but a lot of my recipes were inspired by all of you. I can't say thank you enough, nor express how much I truly appreciate your honesty and realness. When it came to being told if your taste buds didn't agree with all of the flavors I mixed together, if something was too wet or too dry, or was insipid, you all would put it on the wood. I can't say it enough, so once again: thank you all for sharing with me your words of wisdom, love, joy for cooking, and the joy I feel when making others happy through my cooking.

To all who have ordered this book, I truly want you to know that I sincerely appreciate you. When you make any one of the meals as instructed, it should be just like I cooked it for you personally. Once again, "Thank you all," and please enjoy your cookbook, and my love for cooking.

Sincerely,

Calvin L. Brown Jr., aka Big Cal

Notes on Ingredients

In this book, references to "**Ramen**" refer to the Maruchan brand (Japanese) of instant ramen noodles produced by Toyo Suisan Kaisha, Ltd of Tokyo, Japan. References to "**seasoning**" or "**seasoning packs**" are those contained within the noodle packages to produce the flavoring for soup. Maruchan produces over 3.6 billion packages of ramen noodle soup a year. The brand is commonly sold in prisons across the United States.

"**Packs of Ketchup**" refers to the small packets of tomato ketchup often distributed by fast-food restaurants and prison cafeterias. Tomato ketchup, also known as catsup, ketchup, catchup, red sauce, and tomato sauce, is a sauce used as a condiment. The Market leader in the United States (60% market share) and the United Kingdom (82%) is Heinz. Hunt's has the second biggest share of the US market with less than 20%. In much of the UK, ketchup is also known as "tomato sauce" (a term that means a fresher pasta sauce elsewhere in the world) or "red sauce" (especially in Wales).

"**Butter pats**" are small squares (roughly 1" x 1") of margarine/butter/oleo, an individual square cut from a quarter-pound stick of commercial butter. Usually distributed wrapped in wax or foil paper.

"**Sweeteners**" are small packets of sugar substitutes, such as Saccharin or Aspartame.

Brand Names and Food Vendors

Brand names and distributors for food products used in this cookbook come from the Wisconsin state prison canteen (commissary/store) list, as follows:

Legendary Beef Summer Sausage is distributed by Food Express USA, Rancho Dominguez, CA.

These are the items that are made by Back Country and are distributed by Food Express USA: Back Country Bacon, Chicken

Pouch, Chili with Beans, Pre-Sliced Pepperoni, Cappuccino, Instant Milk, Hot Fries, Hot Cheese Nibbles.

These are items made and distributed by Food Express USA: Instant Rice Premium Select, Bee-Happy Honey, Pure Strawberry Preserves, Sayulita Butter Flavor Tortillas, Sayulita Jalapeños, Food Express Colombian Blend Coffee, Food Express 100% Colombian Freeze Dried Coffee, Food Express Premium Pizza Sauce, Food Express Coffee Creamer, Food Express Pure Granulated Sugar, Siam Sweet and Hot Asian Hot Sauce, Fisherman's Paradise - Fish Steaks and Green Chilies, Mackerel, Sardines, Señor Toma's Sharp Cheddar Squeeze Cheese, Coyote Valley Tangy BBQ Chips, Sour Cream and Onion/ Nacho Cheese Chips.

Old Fashioned Cheese, Squeeze Salsa, by Old Fashioned Foods, Inc. Mayville, Wisconsin

Tapa Rosa Nacho Cheese with Jalapeños Dip, Squeeze Ranch Salad Dressing, Eastview Farms Sharp Cheddar, Bacon Jalapeño Cheddar Cheese Bars, Spice Supreme Seasoning Salt, and Garlic, by Gel Spice Co. Inc., Bayonne, NY

Fast Start Breakfast Bar, by McKee Foods, Collegedale, TN

Starlight Mints, Atomic Fire Balls, Lemon Drops, Red Licorice, Root Beer Barrels, and Butterscotch Buttons by Gracey's Goodies

Mr. Nature Roasted Salted Peanuts, Cerritos, CA

Home Brand BBQ Sauce, by The Carriage House Companies

Louisiana Supreme Hot Sauce, by Peppers Unlimited, St. Martinsville, LA

Pepe's Estilo Casero Pork Rinds, Rudolph Foods Lima, OH

Sugar-Free Kool-Aid, Wyler's Tea with Lemon, Lemonade, and Hawaiian Punch, by The Jel Sert Co. Chicago, IL

Sunny D Orange Drink and Microwave Popcorn – Act II Butter Lovers, by Conagra, Chicago, IL

Cook Quik Beans and Rice, by Trinidad Benhem Corp, Denver, CO

Doritos Nachos, Cheetos, and Frito's Corn Chips, Frito-Lay, Inc

Lil' Dutch Maid, Duplex and Peanut Butter Cookies, and Vanilla Wafers, by Abimar Foods, TX

Swiss Miss Classics Hot Cocoa with Marshmallows, by Conagra Foods, Omaha, NE

Mountain Dew, Pepsi, Sierra Mist, Sprite, Reese's Peanut Butter Cups, Milky Way, M&M Peanut, Snickers, Hershey Chocolate Bar, Instant Oatmeal Reg, Variety, and Cinnamon by Ralston Foods, St. Louis, MO

Chocolate Chip Cookies by Checkers Cookies, Biscomerica Corp., CA

Baker's Harvest Graham Crackers, Honey, by Treehouse Private Brands, Inc., Oak Brook, IL

Halal Beef Summer Sausage by Midamar, Midamaf Corp, Cedar Rapids, Iowa, USA

Mrs. Freshley's Swiss Rolls and Buddy Bars, by Flowers Foods, Tucker, GA

Granola Bars Chocolate Chip by Schwlze and Barch Biscuit, IL

Tito's Pickle, New Braunfels, TX.

Saltine Crackers, by Lil' Dutch Maid, Manufactured by Abimar Foods, Inc.

Berry Colossal Crunch Cereal, made by Malt O Meal, Post Consumer Brands, LLC, Lakeville, MN

Generic Premium Tea Bags, made by Food Express USA

Sweetmate Blue artificial sweetener is made by Merisant Company – Merisant US, Inc., Chicago, IL

About the Author

Calvin L. Brown is also known in prison as Big Cal, Big Hershey, Big Finesse, and Mr. Smooth Talker. He is a big dude, 6'4", 380 lbs., with a big personality, a big smile, and a big heart. He is a stylish man of great poise, with an unforgettable sense of humor, who loves making others laugh, just as much as he loves to cook.

As a young boy, he was always amazed when his mother was in her favorite place, her cooking heaven, her kitchen. When she was there, her cooking quintessence was so clearly displayed and catchable. He is eternally grateful to his mama, Lelo, whom he loves and misses dearly. "I thank God every day for the gift of you," Brown says.

While in his own cooking heaven at home, Brown loves to listen to jazz. He believes it allows him to hear the food he's preparing, which he has come to realize is a part of his cooking gift.

Calvin Brown

Summary

This book gives those who are locked down a chance to enjoy great-tasting food again. The recipes came from an extreme man, Calvin L. Brown, who has an unbelievable desire for cooking.

All of the dishes were created and brought to life over years of doing time and hearing others complain about missing out on the finer things in life, like eating out at some of the best eateries.

One day, Mr. Brown said, "Enough is enough!" and decided to allow his love for cooking to be shared. He took his knowledge of cooking from the free world and combined it with all of the ingredients and avenues that he had available in prison to create fine eating for inmates.

His recipes are easy to follow and quick to make, ranging in price for ingredients from $5.00 to $11.00 – very affordable. They are simple and definitely worth one's time to make. Every recipe in this book has been prepared by Cal personally and repeatedly, until perfected.

Reviews

I've been incarcerated for the past 30 years. I've sampled some of the best and some of the worst, so believe me when I tell you that Big Cal's recipes are a cut above the best.
– Mr. Clinton "Silk" Sims

I have done time in 6 different joints in the state of Wisconsin, and I have to tell you, hands down, Big Cal's cooking has been the best I've come across yet! This dude is something else!
– Mr. Justin Rathsack

I've tasted many different types of food from people who say, "I can cook," only to be disappointed. Then Big Cal comes along and makes these brownies that taste like home, the kind your gramma makes for the holidays. My compliments to the chief.
– Mr. Paul Lewis

Say, big homie, I made a banana pudding a few weeks ago, and I remembered you showed me how to make it. Thank you, Big Cal. Much love.
– Mr. Cornelius Carolina

My biggest homie, man, ever since they moved me, I've only been cooking my fried rice and chicken the way you showed me, but now I add just a little cheese. Man, did you give me some game when you showed me how to cook these few dishes? Good looking, big homie.
– Mr. Timothy Gibson

To my surprise, I have never known anybody to mix the flavors of lemon and blueberry. When my big homie Cal did it, I fell in love with his desserts. The recipe was for cookie bars. Never has anyone I have known made such a great combo with those two flavors. To me, he's one of the greatest of all time to the chef a meal. Much love and praise for the big homie!
– Dennis Torres

So, yes, Big Cal, what can I say? He is the top chef here in 2c. He's made his Callzillà for me, and he makes Ramen noodles that

taste better than anybody out there. His desserts – wow, what can I say … the big man has talent.
– Greg Bremer

What's good, big homie? I see you made it to the top; that's what's happening. But on the real deal, the cheesecakes you make, make you want to slap yo mama. Let me know when everything is going well so I can come and get me some more. Stay up, my big dude.
– Mr. Edwin Johnson

From a limited variety of products to skillfully and masterfully create a dish is a delicacy within itself. Big Cal, you've got what it takes to make it.
– Mr. Allee Boone

From my experience with Cal's cooking, I can say firsthand that both his cooking and baking are excellent. Great flavors, best in the compound.
– Tay

I've tasted the Calzillà burrito and some of his desserts. I can say that they are very tasteful, and I will enjoy them until I am gone for sure.
– Midnight

I ate some of his baked macaroni and cheese with chicken and sausage. On a scale of 1 to 10, I'll give it a 10 1/2.
– Mr. James Jackson

The big guy made me a pizza when I first got to S-C-I, and it tasted like it was homemade. Big Cal can work a pack of tortillas. He's a damn good cook.
– Ducky.

Truly the apex of culinary excellence. Prison cuisine is like creating Frankenstein, and this man has perfected his monster.
– Tee

The best cake-, cookie-, pie-maker, hands down. Nobody can make a better dessert than Big Cal!
– 6ix 5ive

This dude is c-r-a-z-y. I don't know how he puts this $#%! together. He must just lay his big ask-questions-self on the bunk thinking $#%! up all day."
– Richie Rich

Cal Brown knows how to cook in a microwave. He is a very creative cook and does perfect work. With his cakes and meals, I believe he could make his own prison cooking show on how to make food in the microwave. Wow, it's very good.
– Big Bull

After eating several of my lil' dude's hook-ups, I can truly say that he got the jailhouse hook-ups on lock! And for the ones I had the pleasure of eating – my favorite is the Callzillà, big boy burrito – keep doing you lil' dude – you know I love to eat also. lol.
– Old School BJ

The Callzillà, aka big boy burrito, was the best damn burrito I ever had in my life! One out of 10, I'm gonna give it 100%, very good.
– Quise

The sweet and spicy cornbread tamales are one of the most creative, tasty creations I've had since being incarcerated. All the flavors work together to form a party on your tongue. Hands down, this is a must-use recipe.
– Twon

Put it like this, Big Cal only makes cheesecakes one time a year for me, and that's on my birthday. I get so many, I named my favorite one Snickers Doodle, N.B.S. I'm a believer when they say "When you want to make shit to sugar, call the Big guy Cal."
– Emmanuel R. Hamilton

I have tried a lot of Big Cal's food, and let me tell you it was some of the best stuff I've eaten in a long time.
– Krazy

The stuff Big Cal makes is off the chain, especially that Big Cal's mud pie.
– Binky

I like the way he develops flavor from such simple ingredients. I believe being able to create such flavorless items from a prison canteen is a gift and the making of a great chef.
– C.G

I've known Mr. Cal Brown for over 10 years. I'm a very picky eater, and I had previously tried many different recipes, to no avail. ... The recipes that I tried from Mr. Brown are good enough that I am now one of his loyal believers.
– Mr. G

This is my very first time in prison, and after Big Cal introduced me to his Callzillà, my way of eating in an institution changed forever. This is a recipe that I will take home and let the wife and kids try. The Big Callzillà sets me free through every bite. Thanks, Big Cal.
– Mr. Jariel Riley

I have to be honest, Big Cal can cook. He just doesn't put everything in a bowl; he takes his time and does things right. He's clean and honest. In the free world, I would buy his food! Keep doing what you do, big homie.
– Joe Blow, from the Go.

He is one of the best; he was born for this. He is passionate about this, "and this is his true calling."
– Mr. Darnell Price

Have you ever had different flavors burst, one after another, in your mouth? My big roadie will surprise you when it comes to food. You wouldn't understand it unless you had had the chance to check him out.
– Anthony Arnold

I have tasted a few of Cal's meals and desserts. I have to admit they were some of the best I have eaten in the 11 years I have been in the Wisconsin DOC. Great job, keep up the good work.
– Carl B.

He is always on top of everything he does. This man has a passion for cooking. All the food in prison that I've tasted from him was beyond excellent. Now imagine what he can do beyond these

bars. He is destined to be great.
– Mr. J Jeter.

I've been locked up for over ten years. I have tasted different inmates' food over time, but none of it compares to Big Cal's. His food tasted so good that it brought me great joy. It gives me a small taste of freedom. I'm talking about there were times when I was angry and down, and I asked Big Cal to cook me something to eat. I'm honestly telling the world that Big Cal's food helped me forget about what I was going through.
– Yo Lucky from the Chi

Never trust a skinny chef! Big Cal's cooking, from desserts to main dishes and everything in between, is five stars. Best variety down to sauces and toppings that make any simple meal taste amazing. This is a must-have prison cookbook.
– Buck

Message to the world and prison system: My name is Thomas Freeland, better known as "Free" to my fellow inmates. I want to let you know that I had the pleasure of tasting the work of Big Cal, and I am a huge fan of his master pieces. They are very tasty, easy to do, and well put together. I told him that he has a gift, and I promise you that you will agree. Not only the taste of it, but the presentation of it all is mind-blowing. I've known him to be a very clean and dedicated individual to his work. So, I give my best to the big homie and much success on his book.
– Lil Homie Free

Mr. Brown's balance of flavors and texture with every meal, as well as dessert, brings you a taste of life that is hard to believe came from a guy using simple things in prison. Food not only supports and nourishes life, but it also gives it a level of love and ecstasy. When done with the steady hands of love and tenderness, it touches your very soul. In my 22 years in prison, I've been around many good chefs, but not like Mr. Brown. His skill with food can only be described as a gift from God for kings. Mr. Brown is ahead of his time. I have tasted every meal of his, and I am his biggest critic, next to himself – I'm not just talking because I know him. Food for me is about the texture. Flavors can easily be manipulated, but texture must be nurtured. Texture brings flavors into balance with your palate. Mr. Brown gives your palate a taste of life. He cooks with joy, love, and wonderment of awe.

– Mr. Marc Rollins

FREEBIRD PUBLISHERS

Thanks for your interest in Freebird Publishers!

We value our customers and would love to hear from you! Reviews are an important part in bringing you quality publications. We love hearing from our readers-rather it's good or bad (though we strive for the best)!

If you could take the time to review/rate any publication you've purchased with Freebird Publishers we would appreciate it!

If your loved one uses Amazon, have them post your review on the books you've read. This will help us tremendously, in providing future publications that are even more useful to our readers and growing our business.

Amazon works off of a 5 star rating system. When having your loved one rate us be sure to give them your chosen star number as well as a written review. Though written reviews aren't required, we truly appreciate hearing from you.

Sample Review Received on Inmate Shopper

poeticsunshine

★★★★★ **Truly a guide**
Reviewed in the United States on June 29, 2023
Verified Purchase

This book is a powerhouse of information. My son had to calm/ground himself to prioritize where to start.

189

FREEBIRD PUBLISHERS
Cook Books

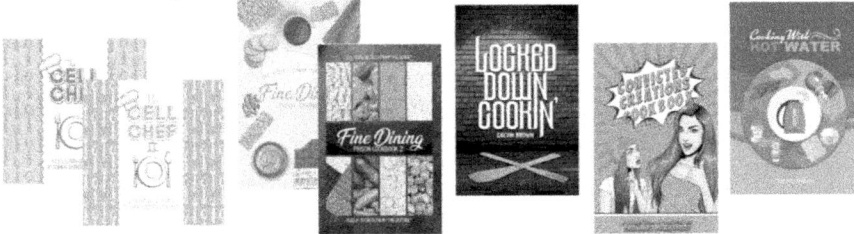

Cell Chef I: Eating the same thing day in and out? Tired of the same boring, bland tasting food? Cell Chef is filled with hundreds of fantastic recipes, simply made with everyday common commissary/store foods. - Meals, Snacks, Sauces, Spreads, Dips, Drinks, Sweet Desserts **$18.99**
Cell Chef II: Completely different and yummier than the past - all new recipes in the Cell Chef's second book. Includes Meals, spreads, sandwiches, sauces, dips, drinks and sweets. **$18.99**
Cell Chef Bundle: Get Cell Chef I and Cell Chef II for the great deal of **$34.98**

Fine Dining 1: Developed by prisoners for prisoners. Cook a delicous, tasty meal with ordinary low-cost ingredients. Tasty drinks, condiments, dips, side dishes, snacks, gumbos, chowders, meals, pizzas, mexican delights, cakes and pies, cheesecakes, and sweets of all kinds. **$20.99**
Fine Dining 2: Ready to be the talk of your unit and discover your creative side at the same time. Over 250 exciting and fun ways to create whatever you're craving in Fine Dining's second book. Including Drinks, dips, soups, beef, chicken, fish, mexican, pizzas, breakfast, pies, cakes, treats, fudge, cookies, pudding and so much more. Bonus content included. **$25.99**
Fine Dining Bundle: Fine Dining 1 and 2. Two great books at a great cost. Only **$41.98**

Locked Down Cookin': A culinary touch on prison commissary and prison meal trays. Culinary touch, "The Big Cal Way." **$20.99**

Convicted Creations Cook Book: Just because you're behind bars, doesn't mean your cravings for home-cooked foods are any less real. With these recipes you'll be able to enjoy the flavors of a good meal. Includes: Drinks, Dips. Sauces, Main Dishes, Sweets and Treats! **$19.99**

Cooking With Hot Water: Tired of prison cookbooks that require a microwave, stinger, hotplate, or any other cooking device? The only thing needed for the recipes in this book is hot (190°) water. Recipe categories include: Drinks, sauces, dips, rice dishes, ramon dishes, bagels, snacks, pizza, mexican food, asian dishes, desserts, frostings, and so much more! **$25.99**

No Order Form Needed: Clearly write on paper & send book name with payment to:

Freebird Publishers 221 Pearl St., Ste. 541, North Dighton, MA 02764
Diane@FreebirdPublishers.com   www.Freebirdpublishers.com
We accept all forms of payment. Plus Venmo & CashApp!
Venmo: @FreebirdPublishers   CashApp: $FreebirdPublishers

www.ingramcontent.com/pod-product-compliance
Lightning Source LLC
Chambersburg PA
CBHW071959090426
42740CB00011B/2014